Table of Contents

Answer Key

www.mathproject.us | 1-844-628-4243

Math Fundamentals: 120 Days of Practice

This book provides the necessary math foundation for middle school students (Grades 6 to 8) before advancing to high school. It is also a great resource for high school students who are looking to polish their foundational math skills. Most calculations in this book can be done using a pencil and paper. Students are encouraged to show their steps as indicated in examples provided at the beginning of each topic (Answer Key Included).

Prerequisite: The content of this book, including practice questions, assumes that the reader is familiar with basic numerical operations, such as multiplication, simple division, addition and subtraction at <u>Grade 4 level</u>. For more information and practice on math fundamentals, please contact us: www.mathproject.us

Use of calculator: We recommend that you do <u>NOT use the calculator</u> while performing calculations and show all your steps. Use the answer key provided to check your answers after the entire worksheet is completed in one sitting.

How to use the book for best results: Each section of the math book begins with lessons that include step-by-step instructions, examples and practice questions. For best results, complete each worksheet in one sitting and note the amount of time it took you in the top right section. If you find yourself struggling to complete any worksheet in more minutes than the number of questions in that worksheet, you need more practice. You may register for the MathProject Club to submit work for detailed feedback, grading and assessment. **Please call us at 1-844-628-4243.**

Leave us a review!

Thank you for choosing MathProject! We'd love to hear your feedback
By leaving us a review, **you allow us to teach more students!**

Fraction Multiplication
Cross Reduction

Why do we cross reduce? Simple!

By cross reducing we are able to make the numbers in the numerator and denominator smaller. This means that we will be multiplying smaller numbers and we will end up with the reduced fraction at the end.

After cross reducing, we multiply the numerators together and the denominators together.

$$\frac{^3\cancel{9}}{_5\cancel{10}} \times \frac{\cancel{4}^2}{\cancel{15}_5} \quad \leftarrow \text{Cross reduce 4 \& 10}$$
$$\leftarrow \text{Cross reduce 9 \& 15}$$

$$= \frac{3}{5} \times \frac{2}{5}$$

$$= \frac{6}{25}$$

Multiply the fractions by cross reducing.

1) $\frac{2}{5} \times \frac{9}{10}$

2) $\frac{5}{6} \times \frac{2}{3}$

3) $\frac{15}{16} \times \frac{5}{12}$

4) $\frac{3}{2} \times \frac{3}{6}$

5) $\frac{16}{21} \times \frac{10}{21}$

6) $\frac{3}{4} \times \frac{4}{5}$

7) $\frac{2}{3} \times \frac{5}{8}$

8) $\frac{2}{3} \times \frac{8}{9}$

9) $\frac{3}{8} \times \frac{3}{4}$

10) $\frac{9}{21} \times \frac{3}{7}$

11) $\frac{4}{7} \times \frac{5}{7}$

12) $\frac{9}{20} \times \frac{7}{12}$

13) $\frac{9}{10} \times \frac{10}{21}$

14) $\frac{6}{7} \times \frac{15}{28}$

15) $\frac{3}{6} \times \frac{9}{24}$

16) $\frac{9}{26} \times \frac{3}{10}$

17) $\frac{3}{7} \times \frac{11}{12}$

18) $\frac{16}{15} \times \frac{25}{32}$

19) $\frac{7}{27} \times \frac{3}{5}$

20) $\frac{2}{21} \times \frac{3}{10}$

21) $\frac{18}{55} \times \frac{44}{81}$

22) $\frac{9}{11} \times \frac{13}{45}$

23) $\frac{5}{8} \times \frac{13}{15}$

24) $\frac{7}{20} \times \frac{30}{49}$

Fraction Multiplication
Whole Number by Fraction
Fraction by Whole Number

We need to know how to multiply fractions and whole numbers. It is very simple!

Step 1:
Rewrite the whole number as a fraction with a denominator of 1.

Step 2:
Cross reduce if possible.

Step 3:
Multiply the fractions.

$$\frac{9}{1} \times \frac{4}{5} \leftarrow \text{Whole numbers have a denominator of 1}$$

$$= \frac{36}{5} \leftarrow \text{Reduce if possible}$$

Multiply and cross reduce when possible.

1) $5 \times \frac{7}{6}$

2) $6 \times \frac{1}{7}$

3) $4 \times \frac{2}{3}$

4) $50 \times \frac{3}{16}$

5) $\frac{23}{24} \times 10$

6) $\frac{9}{22} \times 11$

7) $20 \times \frac{5}{8}$

8) $5 \times \frac{9}{22}$

9) $2 \times \frac{19}{24}$

10) $30 \times \frac{5}{17}$

11) $5 \times \frac{2}{5}$

12) $\frac{3}{4} \times 30$

13) $\frac{2}{3} \times 10$

14) $\frac{4}{7} \times 4$

15) $\frac{7}{12} \times 6$

16) $\frac{5}{16} \times 20$

MATHPROJECT
Empowering minds

Fraction Multiplication
Fraction by Fraction

Step 1: Cross reduce if possible.

Step 2: Multiply the fractions.

Step 3: Check that your final answer is reduced.

$$\frac{4}{7} \times \frac{5}{9}$$ ← Can't cross reduce so we multiply

$$= \frac{20}{63}$$ ← Reduce if possible

Multiply and cross reduce when possible.

1) $\frac{5}{7} \times \frac{7}{9}$

2) $\frac{4}{19} \times \frac{1}{2}$

3) $\frac{2}{3} \times \frac{1}{12}$

4) $\frac{4}{11} \times \frac{1}{6}$

5) $\frac{3}{4} \times \frac{1}{2}$

6) $\frac{4}{5} \times \frac{9}{25}$

7) $\frac{1}{2} \times \frac{4}{11}$

8) $\frac{4}{6} \times \frac{5}{6}$

9) $\frac{21}{22} \times \frac{1}{5}$

10) $\frac{6}{11} \times \frac{5}{6}$

11) $\frac{1}{10} \times \frac{3}{4}$

12) $\frac{1}{6} \times \frac{2}{9}$

13) $\frac{6}{13} \times \frac{12}{14}$

14) $\frac{4}{11} \times \frac{13}{16}$

15) $\frac{11}{22} \times \frac{1}{4}$

Fraction Multiplication

Score:
___/___

Time:
___ : ___

Step 1: Change whole numbers to fractions.
Cross reduce if possible.

Step 2: Multiply the fractions.

Step 3: Check that your final answer is reduced.

$$\frac{1}{\underset{2}{6}} \times \frac{\overset{1}{3}}{4} \quad \leftarrow \text{Cross reduce}$$

$$= \frac{1}{2} \times \frac{1}{4}$$

$$= \frac{1}{8}$$

Multiply and cross reduce when possible.

1) $6 \times \dfrac{12}{25}$

2) $\dfrac{8}{11} \times \dfrac{1}{2}$

3) $20 \times \dfrac{8}{23}$

4) $\dfrac{1}{8} \times \dfrac{1}{10}$

5) $11 \times \dfrac{7}{12}$

6) $\dfrac{2}{11} \times \dfrac{1}{4}$

7) $\dfrac{2}{11} \times 44$

8) $\dfrac{2}{15} \times \dfrac{3}{10}$

9) $14 \times \dfrac{3}{4}$

10) $\dfrac{21}{25} \times \dfrac{8}{15}$

11) $\dfrac{14}{27} \times \dfrac{33}{50}$

12) $\dfrac{12}{49} \times \dfrac{35}{42}$

13) $15 \times \dfrac{11}{20}$

14) $\dfrac{2}{20} \times 5$

MATHPROJECT
Empowering minds

Fraction Multiplication
Fraction by Fraction

Score: __/__

Time: ___ : ___

Step 1:	Step 2:	Step 3:	Step 4:
Change whole numbers to fractions with denominator of 1.	Cross reduce if possible.	Multiply the fractions.	Check that your final answer is reduced.

Multiply and cross reduce when possible.

1) $\dfrac{1}{4} \times \dfrac{1}{3}$

2) $\dfrac{11}{12} \times \dfrac{2}{7}$

3) $\dfrac{3}{4} \times \dfrac{3}{5}$

4) $\dfrac{1}{9} \times \dfrac{11}{12}$

5) $\dfrac{7}{10} \times \dfrac{3}{11}$

6) $\dfrac{1}{6} \times \dfrac{8}{9}$

7) $\dfrac{3}{4} \times \dfrac{6}{7}$

8) $\dfrac{5}{9} \times \dfrac{3}{5}$

9) $\dfrac{1}{5} \times \dfrac{10}{11}$

10) $\dfrac{1}{4} \times \dfrac{3}{11}$

11) $\dfrac{3}{4} \times \dfrac{20}{23}$

12) $\dfrac{13}{15} \times \dfrac{3}{5}$

Step 1: Convert mixed fractions into improper fractions.

Step 2: Cross reduce if possible.

Step 3: Multiply the fractions.

Step 4: Check that your final answer is reduced.

$$2\frac{3}{5} \times 1\frac{4}{5}$$ ← Convert mixed fractions into improper fractions

$$= \frac{13}{5} \times \frac{9}{5}$$ ← Cross reduce if possible

$$= \frac{117}{25}$$

Multiply and cross reduce when possible.

1) $1\frac{1}{5} \times 2\frac{1}{3}$

2) $2\frac{2}{13} \times 5\frac{1}{4}$

3) $1\frac{4}{7} \times 4\frac{3}{4}$

4) $3\frac{4}{7} \times 1\frac{11}{12}$

5) $2\frac{3}{7} \times 3\frac{1}{15}$

6) $3\frac{7}{8} \times 2\frac{1}{10}$

7) $1\frac{6}{7} \times \frac{13}{16}$

8) $1\frac{7}{10} \times \frac{7}{9}$

9) $5\frac{2}{6} \times \frac{3}{17}$

10) $10\frac{4}{5} \times \frac{1}{7}$

11) $30\frac{1}{3} \times \frac{5}{15}$

12) $3\frac{4}{7} \times \frac{1}{17}$

13) $2\frac{7}{8} \times \frac{1}{4}$

14) $2\frac{3}{4} \times \frac{13}{20}$

15) $11\frac{4}{9} \times \frac{1}{5}$

MATHPROJECT
Empowering minds

Fraction Multiplication

Step 1:	Step 2:	Step 3:	Step 4:
Convert all mixed fractions into improper fractions. Change whole numbers into fractions.	Cross reduce if possible.	Multiply the fractions.	Check that your final answer is reduced.

Multiply and cross reduce when possible.

1) $\dfrac{6}{7} \times \dfrac{13}{16}$

2) $\dfrac{7}{10} \times \dfrac{7}{9}$

3) $\dfrac{4}{8} \times \dfrac{7}{7}$

4) $\dfrac{2}{9} \times \dfrac{3}{4}$

5) $\dfrac{1}{7} \times \dfrac{4}{9}$

6) $\dfrac{4}{5} \times \dfrac{1}{4}$

7) $\dfrac{3}{17} \times \dfrac{13}{15}$

8) $\dfrac{1}{3} \times \dfrac{5}{8}$

9) $\dfrac{2}{19} \times \dfrac{5}{16}$

10) $\dfrac{6}{7} \times \dfrac{1}{3}$

11) $2\dfrac{6}{7} \times 2\dfrac{1}{3}$

12) $\dfrac{2}{3} \times 3\dfrac{3}{4}$

13) $1\dfrac{5}{9} \times 2\dfrac{7}{10}$

14) $5\dfrac{8}{5} \times \dfrac{3}{14}$

Fraction Division
Without Cross Reduction

When we divide by a fraction $\frac{a}{b}$, what we are actually doing is multiplying by the reciprocal which is $\frac{b}{a}$. Use these easy steps to remember how to divide fractions.

Step 1: Keep the first fraction the same.

Step 2: Change the division sign into a multiplication sign.

Step 3: Find the reciprocal of the second fraction by flipping it.

Step 4: Multiply the fractions.

$$\frac{7}{10} \div \frac{4}{9}$$

Keep	Change	Flip
$\frac{7}{10}$	x	$\frac{9}{4}$

$$= \frac{63}{40}$$

Divide the following fractions.

1) $\frac{3}{8} \div \frac{1}{3}$

2) $\frac{1}{7} \div \frac{2}{5}$

3) $\frac{1}{3} \div \frac{5}{11}$

4) $\frac{3}{4} \div \frac{1}{2}$

5) $\frac{1}{6} \div \frac{4}{5}$

6) $\frac{1}{3} \div \frac{5}{13}$

7) $\frac{1}{4} \div \frac{8}{9}$

8) $\frac{1}{13} \div \frac{5}{18}$

9) $\frac{7}{15} \div \frac{3}{4}$

10) $\frac{1}{2} \div \frac{5}{7}$

11) $\frac{5}{6} \div \frac{2}{5}$

12) $\frac{5}{12} \div \frac{6}{15}$

13) $\frac{8}{15} \div \frac{12}{15}$

14) $\frac{5}{13} \div \frac{1}{2}$

15) $\frac{3}{5} \div \frac{5}{7}$

16) $\frac{1}{8} \div \frac{1}{5}$

17) $\frac{3}{13} \div \frac{2}{9}$

18) $\frac{10}{13} \div \frac{11}{12}$

Step 1:	Step 2:	Step 3:	Step 4:
Keep the first fraction the same.	Change the division sign into a multiplication sign.	Find the reciprocal of the second fraction by flipping it.	Multiply the fractions.

Divide the following fractions.

1) $\dfrac{5}{8} \div \dfrac{7}{11}$

2) $\dfrac{5}{6} \div \dfrac{2}{5}$

3) $\dfrac{1}{6} \div \dfrac{11}{13}$

4) $\dfrac{5}{10} \div \dfrac{5}{7}$

5) $\dfrac{5}{25} \div \dfrac{13}{15}$

6) $\dfrac{3}{13} \div \dfrac{2}{3}$

7) $\dfrac{1}{4} \div \dfrac{2}{3}$

8) $\dfrac{5}{11} \div \dfrac{1}{2}$

9) $\dfrac{3}{7} \div \dfrac{1}{4}$

10) $\dfrac{5}{12} \div \dfrac{2}{5}$

11) $\dfrac{5}{9} \div \dfrac{2}{7}$

12) $\dfrac{11}{12} \div \dfrac{12}{11}$

13) $\dfrac{6}{7} \div \dfrac{7}{9}$

14) $\dfrac{16}{21} \div \dfrac{3}{4}$

15) $\dfrac{3}{22} \div \dfrac{2}{15}$

16) $\dfrac{10}{33} \div \dfrac{3}{10}$

17) $\dfrac{2}{13} \div \dfrac{7}{10}$

18) $\dfrac{6}{11} \div \dfrac{11}{15}$

Fraction Division
Single Cross Reduction

Step 1: Keep the first fraction the same.
Change the division sign into a multiplication sign.
Flip the second fraction.

Step 2: Cross reduce.

Step 3: Multiply the fractions

$$\frac{5}{11} \div \frac{3}{22} = \frac{5}{11} \times \frac{22}{3}$$
$$= \frac{5}{1} \times \frac{2}{3}$$
$$= \frac{10}{3}$$

Divide and cross reduce.

1) $\frac{1}{3} \div \frac{2}{15}$

2) $\frac{1}{9} \div \frac{1}{18}$

3) $\frac{1}{6} \div \frac{8}{15}$

4) $\frac{1}{7} \div \frac{4}{5}$

5) $\frac{1}{2} \div \frac{5}{6}$

6) $\frac{3}{4} \div \frac{4}{6}$

7) $\frac{1}{6} \div \frac{3}{4}$

8) $\frac{4}{9} \div \frac{2}{4}$

9) $\frac{1}{2} \div \frac{5}{12}$

10) $\frac{7}{22} \div \frac{5}{6}$

11) $\frac{11}{12} \div \frac{1}{6}$

12) $\frac{1}{3} \div \frac{2}{33}$

13) $\frac{5}{12} \div \frac{9}{16}$

14) $\frac{1}{2} \div \frac{5}{16}$

15) $\frac{8}{15} \div \frac{11}{15}$

16) $\frac{10}{13} \div \frac{5}{11}$

17) $\frac{7}{20} \div \frac{5}{6}$

18) $\frac{14}{23} \div \frac{10}{11}$

MATHPROJECT
Empowering minds

Fraction Division
Double Cross Reduction

Step 1: Keep the first fraction the same.
Change division to multiplication and flip the second fraction.

Step 2: Cross Reduce

Step 3: Multiply

$$\frac{21}{22} \div \frac{7}{8}$$

$$= \frac{{}^{3}21}{22_{11}} \times \frac{8^{4}}{7_{1}}$$

$$= \frac{3}{11} \times \frac{4}{1}$$

$$= \frac{12}{11}$$

Divide and cross reduce.

1) $\frac{9}{10} \div \frac{9}{20}$

2) $\frac{3}{4} \div \frac{3}{5}$

3) $\frac{21}{22} \div \frac{3}{10}$

4) $\frac{5}{8} \div \frac{2}{3}$

5) $\frac{8}{9} \div \frac{5}{12}$

6) $\frac{9}{10} \div \frac{5}{7}$

7) $\frac{5}{6} \div \frac{3}{10}$

8) $\frac{2}{3} \div \frac{3}{20}$

9) $\frac{3}{4} \div \frac{2}{15}$

10) $\frac{3}{4} \div \frac{8}{15}$

11) $\frac{5}{7} \div \frac{9}{15}$

12) $\frac{5}{6} \div \frac{2}{5}$

13) $\frac{5}{6} \div \frac{1}{10}$

14) $\frac{2}{8} \div \frac{2}{5}$

15) $\frac{2}{3} \div \frac{3}{22}$

16) $\frac{3}{4} \div \frac{5}{14}$

17) $\frac{3}{4} \div \frac{9}{20}$

18) $\frac{11}{12} \div \frac{33}{60}$

19) $\frac{14}{15} \div \frac{2}{5}$

20) $\frac{5}{12} \div \frac{15}{48}$

21) $\frac{26}{30} \div \frac{13}{15}$

Fraction Division
Fraction by Whole Number

Step 1: Rewrite the whole number as a fraction with a denominator of 1.

Step 2: <u>Keep</u> the first fraction, <u>change</u> division into multiplication and <u>flip</u> the second fraction.

Step 3: If possible cross reduce, then multiply the fractions.

$$\frac{1}{8} \div \frac{3}{1}$$ ← Whole numbers have a denominator of 1

↓ ↓

$$= \frac{1}{8} \times \frac{1}{3}$$ ← To divide fractions we change the problem to multiplication and flip the second fraction

$$= \frac{1}{24}$$

Divide and cross reduce where possible.

1) $\frac{2}{3} \div 3$

2) $\frac{5}{6} \div 2$

3) $\frac{2}{7} \div 10$

4) $\frac{7}{9} \div 6$

5) $\frac{4}{7} \div 5$

6) $\frac{10}{16} \div 7$

7) $\frac{1}{8} \div 5$

8) $\frac{3}{5} \div 6$

9) $\frac{7}{13} \div 2$

10) $\frac{1}{20} \div 3$

11) $\frac{1}{6} \div 3$

12) $\frac{1}{9} \div 5$

13) $\frac{7}{11} \div 4$

14) $\frac{5}{8} \div 4$

15) $\frac{2}{5} \div 6$

16) $\frac{2}{3} \div 4$

17) $\frac{2}{9} \div 1$

18) $\frac{10}{11} \div 9$

MATHPROJECT
Empowering minds

Fraction Division
Whole Number by Fraction &
Fraction by Whole Number

Day 13

Step 1: Rewrite the whole number as a fraction with a denominator of 1.

$$\frac{3}{1} \div \frac{1}{8}$$

Step 2: <u>Keep</u> the first fraction, <u>change</u> division into multiplication and <u>flip</u> the second fraction.

$$= \frac{3}{1} \times \frac{8}{1}$$

Step 3: If possible cross reduce, then multiply the fractions.

$$= \frac{24}{1} \rightarrow 24$$

Divide and cross reduce where possible.

1) $\frac{1}{8} \div 4$

2) $\frac{1}{3} \div 11$

3) $\frac{1}{2} \div 8$

4) $6 \div \frac{2}{3}$

5) $5 \div \frac{1}{7}$

6) $7 \div \frac{4}{5}$

7) $\frac{1}{2} \div 5$

8) $\frac{2}{5} \div 3$

9) $\frac{1}{3} \div 2$

10) $\frac{2}{7} \div 1$

11) $\frac{2}{6} \div 7$

12) $2 \div \frac{1}{3}$

13) $3 \div \frac{1}{4}$

14) $1 \div \frac{9}{10}$

15) $8 \div \frac{2}{3}$

16) $9 \div \frac{7}{8}$

17) $15 \div \frac{3}{10}$

18) $11 \div \frac{7}{9}$

19) $4 \div \frac{10}{11}$

20) $10 \div \frac{15}{16}$

21) $3 \div \frac{3}{25}$

Fraction Division
One Mixed Fraction & Cross Reduction

Score: __ / __

Time: __ : __

Step 1: Change the mixed fraction into an improper fraction.

Step 2: Find the reciprocal of the second fraction, and change the division to multiplication.

Step 3: If possible cross reduce, then multiply the fractions.

<u>Reciprocal</u>: the fraction obtained by switching the numerator and the denominator. (ie. 4/5 is the reciprocal of 5/4)

$$\frac{1}{3} \div 3\frac{3}{5}$$

$$= \frac{1}{3} \div \frac{18}{5}$$

$$= \frac{1}{3} \times \frac{5}{18}$$

$$= \frac{5}{54}$$

Divide and cross reduce where possible.

1) $\dfrac{7}{8} \div 1\dfrac{3}{7}$

6) $4\dfrac{12}{14} \div \dfrac{7}{12}$

11) $\dfrac{13}{14} \div \dfrac{5}{11}$

2) $\dfrac{5}{16} \div 4\dfrac{1}{12}$

7) $\dfrac{3}{4} \div 8\dfrac{1}{2}$

12) $\dfrac{15}{18} \div 5\dfrac{1}{5}$

3) $\dfrac{3}{10} \div 3\dfrac{1}{6}$

8) $\dfrac{11}{12} \div 7\dfrac{1}{3}$

13) $6\dfrac{3}{6} \div \dfrac{3}{5}$

4) $\dfrac{2}{3} \div 2\dfrac{4}{9}$

9) $\dfrac{15}{16} \div 2\dfrac{3}{8}$

14) $6\dfrac{1}{6} \div \dfrac{7}{12}$

5) $\dfrac{8}{9} \div 1\dfrac{16}{28}$

10) $\dfrac{9}{14} \div 2\dfrac{6}{10}$

15) $10\dfrac{5}{6} \div \dfrac{2}{3}$

Fraction Division
One Mixed Fraction &
Cross Reduction

Step 1: Change the mixed fraction into an improper fraction.

Step 2: Find the <u>reciprocal</u> of the second fraction, and change the division to multiplication.

Step 3: If possible cross reduce, then multiply the fractions.

$$\frac{3}{5} \div 1\frac{9}{15}$$

$$= \frac{3}{5} \div \frac{24}{15}$$

$$= \frac{3}{5} \times \frac{15}{24}$$

$$= \frac{3}{8}$$

Divide and cross reduce where possible.

1) $\frac{1}{18} \div 1\frac{3}{7}$

2) $2\frac{8}{10} \div \frac{2}{5}$

3) $7\frac{1}{6} \div \frac{3}{5}$

4) $\frac{15}{16} \div 1\frac{2}{8}$

5) $\frac{15}{20} \div 2\frac{1}{5}$

6) $3\frac{9}{10} \div \frac{3}{16}$

7) $\frac{1}{6} \div 6\frac{12}{16}$

8) $\frac{1}{2} \div 1\frac{5}{8}$

9) $2\frac{1}{2} \div \frac{1}{4}$

10) $3\frac{3}{4} \div \frac{1}{6}$

11) $\frac{2}{3} \div 1\frac{1}{2}$

12) $10\frac{2}{6} \div \frac{1}{3}$

13) $9\frac{7}{15} \div \frac{1}{2}$

14) $2\frac{8}{15} \div \frac{2}{4}$

15) $4\frac{15}{20} \div \frac{1}{4}$

Fraction Division
One Mixed Fraction &
Cross Reduction

$$4\tfrac{1}{11} \div \tfrac{5}{22}$$ ← Convert the mixed fraction into an improper fraction

$$= \tfrac{45}{11} \div \tfrac{5}{22}$$ ← Flip the divisor and change from ÷ → ×

$$= \tfrac{45}{11} \times \tfrac{22}{5}$$ ← Cross reduce

$$= \tfrac{9}{1} \times \tfrac{2}{1}$$ ← Multiply

$$= 18$$

Divide and cross reduce where possible.

1) $2\tfrac{2}{7} \div \tfrac{9}{10}$

2) $4\tfrac{5}{6} \div \tfrac{3}{5}$

3) $\tfrac{5}{16} \div 3\tfrac{1}{4}$

4) $\tfrac{3}{4} \div 1\tfrac{12}{13}$

5) $\tfrac{7}{8} \div 4\tfrac{1}{4}$

6) $\tfrac{5}{10} \div 10\tfrac{5}{6}$

7) $\tfrac{5}{10} \div 4\tfrac{2}{5}$

8) $\tfrac{2}{3} \div 2\tfrac{1}{6}$

9) $\tfrac{7}{8} \div 1\tfrac{2}{5}$

10) $\tfrac{5}{6} \div 3\tfrac{2}{5}$

11) $\tfrac{6}{12} \div 6\tfrac{2}{4}$

12) $\tfrac{2}{6} \div 1\tfrac{4}{6}$

13) $\tfrac{4}{12} \div 8\tfrac{1}{4}$

14) $\tfrac{2}{3} \div 1\tfrac{8}{11}$

15) $\tfrac{2}{3} \div 3\tfrac{12}{15}$

16) $\tfrac{7}{16} \div 1\tfrac{1}{2}$

17) $\tfrac{2}{13} \div 1\tfrac{1}{3}$

18) $3\tfrac{7}{11} \div \tfrac{4}{5}$

Fraction Division
One Mixed Fraction & Cross Reduction

$\frac{17}{18} \div 1\frac{1}{4}$ ← Convert the mixed fraction into an improper fraction

$= \frac{17}{18} \div \frac{5}{4}$ ← Flip the divisor and change from ÷ → ×

$= \frac{17}{18} \times \frac{4}{5}$ ← Cross reduce

$= \frac{17}{9} \times \frac{2}{5}$ ← Multiply

$= \frac{34}{45}$

Divide and cross reduce where possible.

1) $\frac{4}{14} \div 1\frac{3}{4}$

2) $\frac{1}{6} \div \frac{2}{15}$

3) $\frac{3}{20} \div 2\frac{12}{14}$

4) $9\frac{1}{3} \div \frac{2}{7}$

5) $\frac{2}{9} \div 2\frac{2}{5}$

6) $\frac{1}{2} \div 3\frac{6}{20}$

7) $\frac{4}{5} \div 5\frac{1}{3}$

8) $\frac{1}{2} \div 1\frac{2}{5}$

9) $\frac{5}{6} \div 2\frac{2}{6}$

10) $\frac{1}{2} \div 2\frac{2}{3}$

11) $\frac{1}{6} \div 4\frac{2}{6}$

12) $\frac{2}{3} \div 6\frac{2}{5}$

13) $\frac{3}{20} \div 6\frac{2}{3}$

14) $\frac{8}{10} \div 3\frac{2}{10}$

15) $\frac{15}{18} \div 1\frac{2}{10}$

Fraction Division
Two Mixed Fractions & Cross Reduction

Score: ___/___

Time: ___:___

Step 1: Change the mixed fractions into improper fractions.

Step 2: Find the reciprocal of the second fraction, and change the division to multiplication.

Step 3: If possible cross reduce, then multiply the fractions.

$$1\frac{3}{21} \div 2\frac{2}{3}$$

$$= \frac{24}{21} \div \frac{8}{3}$$

$$= \frac{^3 24}{_7 21} \times \frac{3^{-1}}{8_1}$$

$$= \frac{3}{7}$$

Divide and cross reduce where possible.

1) $1\frac{3}{18} \div 2\frac{3}{7}$

2) $7\frac{2}{8} \div 1\frac{1}{5}$

3) $1\frac{3}{4} \div 4\frac{2}{9}$

4) $2\frac{5}{6} \div 3\frac{2}{5}$

5) $4\frac{3}{8} \div 2\frac{2}{7}$

6) $1\frac{2}{6} \div 3\frac{2}{8}$

7) $1\frac{1}{4} \div 2\frac{5}{6}$

8) $1\frac{3}{8} \div 2\frac{4}{5}$

9) $1\frac{3}{4} \div 1\frac{8}{15}$

10) $1\frac{5}{6} \div 1\frac{2}{5}$

11) $3\frac{6}{10} \div 1\frac{7}{12}$

12) $5\frac{1}{2} \div 7\frac{2}{3}$

13) $1\frac{2}{6} \div 2\frac{3}{7}$

14) $2\frac{4}{12} \div 4\frac{1}{8}$

15) $4\frac{5}{6} \div 3\frac{2}{5}$

MATHPROJECT
Empowering minds

Fraction Division
Two Mixed Fractions & Cross Reduction

Day 19

Step 1: Change the mixed fraction into an improper fraction.

Step 2: Find the reciprocal of the second fraction, and change the division to multiplication.

Step 3: If possible cross reduce, then multiply the fractions.

$$4\frac{2}{5} \div 10\frac{2}{3}$$

$$= \frac{22}{5} \div \frac{32}{3}$$

$$= \frac{\overset{11}{22}}{5} \times \frac{3}{\underset{16}{32}}$$

$$= \frac{33}{80}$$

Divide and cross reduce where possible.

1) $1\frac{5}{8} \div 4\frac{3}{4}$

2) $2\frac{2}{3} \div 3\frac{7}{13}$

3) $2\frac{4}{9} \div 1\frac{2}{3}$

4) $5\frac{3}{5} \div 2\frac{8}{11}$

5) $6\frac{2}{3} \div 1\frac{1}{20}$

6) $5\frac{2}{6} \div 2\frac{3}{7}$

7) $2\frac{5}{6} \div 1\frac{2}{5}$

8) $1\frac{8}{12} \div 3\frac{1}{5}$

9) $2\frac{1}{2} \div 10\frac{2}{8}$

10) $1\frac{4}{6} \div 1\frac{2}{36}$

11) $2\frac{4}{12} \div 5\frac{5}{13}$

12) $3\frac{3}{12} \div 1\frac{5}{10}$

13) $6\frac{4}{12} \div 2\frac{2}{4}$

14) $1\frac{9}{12} \div 1\frac{3}{10}$

15) $2\frac{2}{6} \div 3\frac{5}{10}$

Fraction Division
Two Mixed Fractions & Cross Reduction

Score: ___/___

Time: ___ : ___

$$\frac{17}{18} \div 1\frac{1}{4} \qquad \leftarrow \text{Convert the mixed fraction into an improper fraction}$$

$$= \frac{35}{18} \div \frac{5}{4} \qquad \leftarrow \text{Flip the divisor and change from} \div \rightarrow \times$$

$$= \frac{35}{18} \times \frac{4}{5} \qquad \leftarrow \text{Cross reduce}$$

$$= \frac{7}{9} \times \frac{2}{1} \qquad \leftarrow \text{Multiply}$$

$$= \frac{14}{9}$$

Divide and cross reduce where possible.

1) $2\frac{5}{10} \div 5\frac{5}{18}$

2) $3\frac{2}{6} \div 8\frac{1}{2}$

3) $2\frac{6}{12} \div 6\frac{1}{5}$

4) $6\frac{5}{5} \div 2\frac{5}{15}$

5) $2\frac{2}{10} \div 10\frac{4}{6}$

6) $2\frac{5}{15} \div 1\frac{1}{3}$

7) $7\frac{5}{7} \div 1\frac{12}{14}$

8) $10\frac{2}{8} \div 2\frac{3}{4}$

9) $5\frac{3}{10} \div 2\frac{6}{15}$

Fraction Division
Two Mixed Fractions &
Cross Reduction

$1\frac{1}{6} \div 3\frac{1}{4}$ ← Convert the mixed fraction into an improper fraction

$= \frac{7}{6} \div \frac{13}{4}$ ← Flip the divisor and change from ÷ → ×

$= \frac{7}{6} \times \frac{13}{4}$ ← Can't cross reduce, then multiply

$= \frac{91}{24}$

Divide and cross reduce where possible.

1) $1\frac{3}{12} \div 1\frac{2}{5}$

2) $6\frac{2}{8} \div 3\frac{10}{15}$

3) $2\frac{5}{6} \div 1\frac{2}{3}$

4) $1\frac{5}{12} \div 1\frac{12}{15}$

5) $11\frac{1}{7} \div 12\frac{1}{7}$

6) $4\frac{7}{10} \div 4\frac{6}{12}$

7) $5\frac{8}{16} \div 3\frac{4}{14}$

8) $3\frac{6}{11} \div 2\frac{2}{5}$

9) $5\frac{1}{3} \div 3\frac{1}{5}$

10) $1\frac{1}{3} \div 10\frac{2}{10}$

Fraction Division

$$2\frac{5}{8} \div 1\frac{7}{9} \leftarrow \text{Change into improper fraction}$$

$$= \frac{21}{8} \div \frac{16}{9} \leftarrow \text{Multiply and flip}$$

$$= \frac{21}{8} \times \frac{9}{16}$$

$$= \frac{189}{128}$$

Divide and cross reduce where possible.

1) $2\frac{1}{8} \div 3\frac{3}{6}$

2) $4\frac{5}{6} \div 5\frac{2}{5}$

3) $2\frac{4}{11} \div 1\frac{5}{9}$

4) $\frac{8}{10} \div 5$

5) $\frac{3}{11} \div 2$

6) $\frac{6}{9} \div 8$

7) $2 \div \frac{1}{4}$

8) $10 \div \frac{3}{4}$

9) $3 \div \frac{2}{15}$

10) $2\frac{1}{2} \div \frac{2}{4}$

11) $\frac{8}{13} \div 3\frac{1}{5}$

12) $\frac{5}{7} \div 3\frac{5}{8}$

13) $\frac{2}{6} \div \frac{6}{13}$

14) $\frac{14}{16} \div \frac{7}{13}$

15) $\frac{7}{15} \div \frac{1}{8}$

MATHPROJECT
Empowering minds

Fraction Division
Prime Numbers &
Composite Numbers

Factors are numbers that multiply together to get a specified number. Another way of thinking about it is that factors are the numbers that evenly divide a given number.

For instance the factors of 16 are 1, 2, 4, 8, and 16.

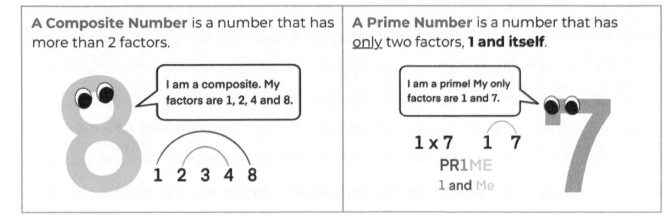

A Composite Number is a number that has more than 2 factors.

I am a composite. My factors are 1, 2, 4 and 8.

1 2 3 4 8

A Prime Number is a number that has only two factors, **1 and itself**.

I am a prime! My only factors are 1 and 7.

1 x 7   1 7

PR1ME

1 and Me

Circle all the prime numbers.

(87)	25	85	62	23
8	26	21	48	98
90	99	40	64	88
73	57	61	85	43
53	35	93	16	101
26	4	93	61	76

Prime Factorization & Factor Trees

Prime factorization is where we write a composite number as a product of prime numbers. To break down a composite number into prime numbers we use factor trees.

Step 1: Write the composite number.

Step 2: Find two numbers, one of them should be a prime number, whose product is the composite and write it directly below.

Step 3: Repeat step 2 for the new composite number until you end up with only a prime number.

Step 4: Write the multiplication statement with your prime numbers.

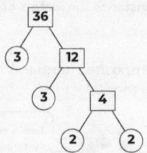

$36 = 3 \times 3 \times 2 \times 2$

or $3^2 \times 2^2$

Using the factor trees, determine the prime factorization of each number.

1)

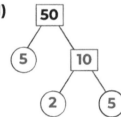

$50 = 2 \times 5 \times 5$

or 2×5^2

2)

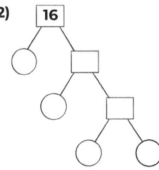

$16 =$

3)

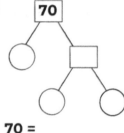

$70 =$

4)

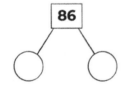

$86 =$

5)

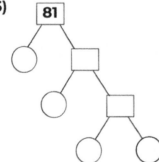

$81 =$

6)

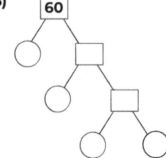

$60 =$

Lowest Common Multiples

Score: __/__

Time: ___:___

A **multiple** is a number product of a given number and another number. They can be found by skip counting. For instance the multiples of 5 are 5, 10, 15, 20, 25, ...

The **lowest common multiple (LCM)** of two or more numbers is the smallest multiple that they have in common. There are a few ways to find the LCM of a group of numbers. Below is one way you can find the LCM.

Start by listing a few multiples of each number and checking to see if they have any common multiple.

If no multiple is found, continue listing more multiples until you find a common one for both.

Number	Multiples
14	14 , 28 , 42 , 56 , **70** , 84 , 98 , 112 , 126 , 140
10	10 , 20 , 30 , 40 , 50, 60 , **70** , 80 , 90 , 100

Find the Lowest Common Multiple for each number pair.

1) 14, 10 __70__

2) 30, 6 _____

3) 15, 20 _____

4) 24, 6 _____

5) 12, 8 _____

6) 5, 20 _____

7) 30, 12 _____

8) 30, 50 _____

9) 13, 4 _____

10) 11, 12 _____

Here is another method for finding the LCM of a set of numbers.

Step 1: Divide by a factor common to both 12 and 16. **(2)**

Step 2: Divide by a factor common to both 6 and 8. **(2)**

Step 3: Continue until the only factor left is 1.

Step 4: Make a "**BIG L**" with the numbers in the left column and bottom row.

TIC-TAC-TOE
Method

2	12	16
2	6	8
1	3	4

Step 5: Take the numbers inside the "**L**" and multiply them to find the LCM.

Find the Lowest Common Multiple for each number pair.

1) 12, 16 __48__

2) 12, 8 ____

3) 32, 12 ____

4) 12, 4 ____

5) 12, 15 ____

6) 7, 16 ____

7) 14, 8 ____

8) 28, 12 ____

9) 120, 210 ____

10) 24, 8 ____

MATHPROJECT
Empowering minds

Listing Factors

Factors are numbers that multiply together to get a specified number. Another way of thinking about it is that factors are the numbers that evenly divide a given number.

The factors of **24** are **1, 2, 3, 4, 6, 8, 12, and 24**.
You can see that the factors pair up to give a product of 24.

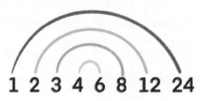

1 2 3 4 6 8 12 24

List all the factors for each number.

1) 14 _____

2) 27 _____

3) 57 _____

4) 88 _____

5) 22 _____

6) 36 _____

7) 20 _____

8) 39 _____

9) 58 _____

10) 63 _____

11) 56 _____

12) 86 _____

13) 25 _____

14) 46 _____

Greatest Common Factor

The **greatest common factor (GCF)** of two or more numbers is the largest factor that they have in common. There are few ways to determine the GCF of a set of numbers. Below is one way to find the GCF.

Start by listing all the factors of each number. The largest factor they have in common is the GCF.

Number	Factors
16	1 , 2 , 4 , **8** , 16
24	1 , 2 , 3 , 4 , 6 , **8** , 12 , 24

Find the Greatest Common Factor for each pair of numbers.

1) 4, 40 _____

2) 30, 8 _____

3) 12, 16 _____

4) 20, 35 _____

5) 45, 54 _____

6) 33, 55 _____

7) 2, 12 _____

8) 90, 75 _____

9) 15, 8 _____

10) 32, 80 _____

MATHPROJECT
Empowering minds

Greatest Common Factor

Here is another method you can use to find the GCF.

Step 1: Divide by a factor common to both 15 and 45. (5)

Step 2: Divide by a factor common to both 3 and 9. (3)

Step 3: Continue until the only factor left is 1.

Step 4: Make a box around the numbers in the left column and multiply them to find the GCF.

5	15	45
3	3	9
1	1	3

GCF: 5 x 3 x 1 = 15

Find the Greatest Common Factor for each number pair.

1) 24, 3 _____

2) 30, 24 _____

3) 45, 81 _____

4) 30, 4 _____

5) 10, 2 _____

6) 39, 65 _____

7) 50, 28 _____

8) 20, 30 _____

9) 15, 10 _____

10) 28, 70 _____

Greatest Common Factor & Lowest Common Multiple

Score: __/__   Time: ___:___

GRASS Method				
G: Given	**R: Required**	**A: Action**	**S: Solve**	**S: Statement**
Write down what information is given in the question.	Write down what you need to find/answer.	Write down how you will solve the question.	Calculate the answer.	State your answer in a full sentence.

For more information on how to solve word problems refer to Appendix A.

Solve the word problems using GRS / GRASS Method.

Questions	Solutions
Macy is making gifts for each of her classmates. She has 45 pencils, 30 gumballs and 15 stickers. If each gift should have the same number of items, how many gifts can she make?	**G:** 45 pencils, 30 gumballs and 15 **R:** stickers find the GCF **S:** Pencils → 45: 1, 3, 5, 9, **15**, 45 Gumballs → 30: 1, 2, 3, 5, 6, 10, **15**, 30 Stickers → 15: 1, 3, 5, **15** Therefore, she can make 15 gifts for her classmates.
1) To become a better shooter, Steph practices free throws every 2 days, three pointers every 4 days, and half court shots every 7 days. If Steph did all three activities today, in how many days will he do all three practices on the same day?	
2) James wants to cook 12 corn, 24 potatoes, and 66 cabbages. If James puts the same amount of vegetables in each pot and each pot has only one type of vegetable, what is the greatest number of vegetables he can put in one pot?	

 MATHPROJECT
Empowering minds

3) Nate needs to ship 16 sports games, 20 platform games, and 10 puzzle games. He
can pack only one type of game in each box and he must pack the same number of games in each box.

What is the greatest number of games Nate can pack in each box?

4) Knives are sold in packages of 3 and forks are sold in packages of 5.

If you want to have the same number of each item, what is the least number of packages of each you need to buy?

5) Taco day occurs every 14 days, if the last Taco Day occurred on a Tuesday.

How many days will until taco day occurs again on a Tuesday?

6) A chef is preparing lunch. There are 9 loaves of bread and 18 cabbages.

If the chef wants all the dishes to be identical, then what is the greatest number of dishes that the chef serves?

Adding Fractions
Mixed Fractions

When it comes to adding fractions we use the following steps.

Step 1: Convert mixed fractions into improper fractions.
Step 2: Each fraction must have the same denominator.
Step 3: Add the numerators and keep the denominator.
Step 4: Reduce when possible.
Step 5: Convert the solution to a mixed number.

$2\frac{2}{5} + 1\frac{1}{2}$ ←Convert mixed fractions to improper fractions

$= \frac{12^{\times 2}}{5_{\times 2}} + \frac{3^{\times 5}}{2_{\times 5}}$ ←Find a common denominator

$= \frac{24}{10} + \frac{15}{10}$ ←Add fractions

$= \frac{39}{10} = 3\frac{9}{10}$ ←You could convert the improper fraction to a mixed number

Add the fractions and give the answer in the form of a mixed fraction.

1) $1\frac{1}{2} + 1\frac{1}{2}$

2) $5\frac{2}{5} + 3\frac{4}{7}$

3) $6\frac{3}{4} + 4\frac{3}{10}$

4) $9\frac{5}{6} + 2\frac{2}{5}$

5) $1\frac{3}{4} + 4\frac{1}{4}$

6) $1\frac{1}{3} + 1\frac{2}{4}$

7) $2\frac{2}{10} + 1\frac{1}{8}$

8) $2\frac{2}{10} + 1\frac{1}{8}$

9) $1\frac{6}{10} + 3\frac{1}{4}$

10) $3\frac{6}{8} + 1\frac{5}{7}$

11) $1\frac{4}{5} + 4\frac{1}{9}$

12) $1\frac{1}{12} + 1\frac{3}{4}$

13) $1\frac{4}{6} + 2\frac{5}{6}$

14) $3\frac{2}{8} + 1\frac{2}{18}$

15) $1\frac{5}{7} + 1\frac{1}{2}$

MATHPROJECT
Empowering minds

Adding Fractions
Mixed Fractions

Here is another method we can use to add fractions.

Step 1: Each fraction must have the same denominator.

Step 2: Add the whole numbers together and add the fractions together.

Step 3: Simplify and reduce if possible.

$2\frac{3^{\times3}}{4_{\times3}} + 3\frac{1^{\times4}}{3_{\times4}}$ — Find a common denominator

$= 2\frac{9}{12} + 3\frac{4}{12}$

Add whole numbers
Add fractions

$= 5\frac{13}{12}$

$= 6\frac{1}{12}$ — Simplify $5 + 1\frac{1}{12}$

Add the fractions and give the answer in the form of a mixed fraction.

1) $2\frac{3}{6} + 3\frac{8}{11}$

6) $6\frac{1}{10} + 3\frac{1}{5}$

2) $3\frac{3}{8} + 4\frac{1}{2}$

7) $7\frac{1}{3} + 3\frac{1}{15}$

3) $4\frac{4}{8} + 1\frac{5}{7}$

8) $3\frac{6}{9} + 2\frac{3}{9}$

4) $2\frac{5}{8} + 1\frac{3}{6}$

9) $1\frac{5}{6} + 3\frac{1}{7}$

5) $1\frac{3}{4} + 1\frac{6}{8}$

10) $3\frac{2}{7} + 1\frac{5}{10}$

Adding Fractions
Mixed Fractions

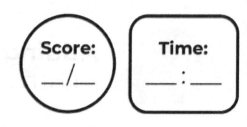
$1\frac{1}{2} + 9\frac{2}{3}$ ← **Convert** mixed fractions to improper fractions

$= \frac{3 \times 3}{2 \times 3} + \frac{27 \times 2}{3 \times 2}$ ← Establish a **common denominator**

$= \frac{9}{6} + \frac{54}{6}$ ← **Add** the numerators and keep the denominator

$= \frac{63}{6}$ ← **Reduce** if possible.

$= \frac{21}{2} = 10\frac{1}{2}$ ← **Convert** the improper fraction to a mixed fraction.

Add the fractions and give the answer in the form of a mixed fraction.

1) $1\frac{7}{10} + 3\frac{2}{6}$

6) $1\frac{5}{7} + 3\frac{2}{4}$

2) $1\frac{4}{5} + 6\frac{1}{3}$

7) $4\frac{10}{17} + 1\frac{1}{3}$

3) $3\frac{2}{10} + 2\frac{3}{12}$

8) $3\frac{8}{9} + 6\frac{1}{6}$

4) $3\frac{3}{8} + 2\frac{1}{7}$

9) $1\frac{10}{15} + 1\frac{6}{8}$

5) $2\frac{1}{18} + 5\frac{1}{3}$

10) $1\frac{7}{14} + 1\frac{1}{8}$

MATHPROJECT
Empowering minds

The same methods we use to add fractions can be used to subtract fractions.

Method 1: Solve as Improper Fractions	Method 2: Solve as Mixed Fractions
$9\frac{1}{8} - 3\frac{1}{3}$ $= \frac{73^{\times 3}}{8^{\times 3}} - \frac{10^{\times 8}}{3^{\times 8}}$ $= \frac{219}{24} - \frac{80}{24}$ $= \frac{139}{24} = 5\frac{19}{24}$	$9\frac{1}{8} - 3\frac{1}{3}$ $= (9-3) + \left(\frac{3}{24} - \frac{8}{24}\right)$ $= 6 + \left(\frac{-5}{24}\right)$ $= \frac{6^{\times 24}}{1^{\times 24}} + \left(\frac{-5}{24}\right)$ $= \frac{144-5}{24} = \frac{139}{24} = 5\frac{19}{24}$

Subtract the fractions and give the answer in the form of a mixed fraction.

1) $9\frac{4}{12} - 3\frac{4}{8}$

2) $3\frac{3}{10} - 1\frac{6}{10}$

3) $5\frac{3}{4} - 3\frac{2}{3}$

4) $3\frac{1}{16} - 1\frac{1}{5}$

5) $1\frac{7}{16} - 1\frac{1}{10}$

6) $3\frac{4}{8} - 2\frac{1}{10}$

7) $13\frac{1}{3} - 5\frac{4}{6}$

8) $2\frac{6}{18} - 2\frac{1}{15}$

9) $9\frac{2}{3} - 1\frac{3}{8}$

10) $7\frac{9}{27} - 4\frac{5}{15}$

11) $9\frac{8}{12} - 3\frac{1}{9}$

12) $5\frac{4}{7} - 1\frac{3}{8}$

13) $3\frac{4}{6} - 1\frac{3}{11}$

14) $4\frac{1}{6} - 3\frac{6}{14}$

15) $4\frac{12}{16} - 3\frac{1}{30}$

16) $1\frac{11}{15} - 1\frac{4}{8}$

17) $1\frac{13}{16} - 1\frac{1}{8}$

18) $10\frac{2}{5} - 4\frac{1}{7}$

19) $3\frac{2}{5} - 2\frac{4}{11}$

20) $2\frac{7}{10} - 2\frac{9}{20}$

21) $9\frac{2}{13} - 4\frac{3}{10}$

22) $7\frac{19}{27} - 6\frac{5}{9}$

23) $5\frac{8}{15} - \frac{1}{10}$

24) $5\frac{4}{9} - 5\frac{1}{8}$

Subtracting Fractions
Mixed Fractions

$2\frac{5}{6} - \frac{1^{\times 2}}{3^{\times 2}}$ ← Let's leave it as mixed fractions and do a **common denominator**.

$= 2\frac{5}{6} - \frac{2}{6}$ ← **Subtract** the whole numbers and then subtract the fractions.

$= 2\frac{3^{\,1}}{6_{\,2}}$ ← **Reduce** if necessary.

$= 2\frac{1}{2}$

Subtract the fractions and give the answer in the form of a mixed fraction.

1) $3\frac{3}{15} - 1\frac{4}{9}$

2) $3\frac{1}{2} - 1\frac{10}{11}$

3) $3\frac{2}{11} - 1\frac{3}{4}$

4) $3\frac{2}{10} - 1\frac{2}{16}$

5) $8\frac{4}{8} - 1\frac{6}{10}$

6) $4\frac{8}{21} - 1\frac{8}{9}$

7) $3\frac{4}{6} - 1\frac{1}{5}$

8) $2\frac{7}{12} - 1\frac{4}{20}$

9) $5\frac{5}{11} - 3\frac{1}{4}$

10) $3\frac{2}{10} - 1\frac{2}{16}$

11) $8\frac{1}{3} - 1\frac{6}{7}$

12) $4\frac{6}{21} - 2\frac{6}{7}$

13) $3\frac{3}{5} - 2\frac{4}{11}$

14) $5\frac{1}{2} - 3\frac{1}{15}$

15) $2\frac{2}{12} - 1\frac{3}{4}$

16) $11\frac{3}{10} - 6\frac{5}{6}$

17) $1\frac{3}{8} - 1\frac{1}{10}$

18) $5\frac{11}{20} - 4\frac{3}{10}$

19) $10\frac{5}{6} - 5\frac{1}{4}$

20) $3\frac{7}{10} - 1\frac{4}{11}$

21) $3\frac{2}{13} - 2\frac{3}{4}$

22) $9\frac{9}{10} - 4\frac{2}{12}$

23) $4\frac{2}{7} - 3\frac{6}{11}$

24) $10\frac{3}{14} - 5\frac{6}{7}$

MATHPROJECT
Empowering minds

Subtracting Fractions
Mixed Fractions

Score: __/__

Time: ___ : ___

Alternative method for the example provided in Day 34, method 2

$$9\frac{1^{\times 3}}{8_{\times 3}} - 3\frac{1^{\times 8}}{3_{\times 8}} = 9\frac{3}{24} - 3\frac{8}{24} = (9-3) + \left(\frac{3}{24} - \frac{8}{24}\right) = 6 + \left(\frac{-5}{24}\right)$$

$$= 6 + \left(\frac{-5}{24}\right) \longleftarrow \text{Write 6 as a mixed number and solve.}$$

$$= 5\frac{24}{24} - \frac{5}{24} = 5\frac{19}{24}$$

Note that:

$$6 = 5 + \frac{1^{\times 24}}{1_{\times 24}} = 5 + \frac{24}{24} = 5\frac{24}{24}$$

Subtract the fractions and give the answer in the form of a mixed fraction.

1) $9\frac{7}{8} - 1\frac{1}{4}$

2) $3\frac{1}{3} - 2\frac{2}{8}$

3) $3\frac{1}{7} - 1\frac{2}{6}$

4) $6\frac{1}{3} - 2\frac{3}{4}$

5) $3\frac{3}{4} - 1\frac{5}{6}$

6) $6\frac{1}{3} - 1\frac{3}{6}$

7) $5\frac{5}{8} - 1\frac{3}{8}$

8) $10\frac{3}{16} - 2\frac{6}{10}$

9) $7\frac{1}{6} - 3\frac{1}{10}$

10) $10\frac{5}{10} - 3\frac{1}{4}$

11) $3\frac{2}{5} - 3\frac{1}{10}$

12) $1\frac{2}{3} - \frac{5}{12}$

13) $4\frac{2}{9} - 2\frac{4}{5}$

14) $3\frac{1}{3} - 1\frac{2}{7}$

15) $3\frac{4}{7} - \frac{2}{11}$

16) $12\frac{7}{9} - 7\frac{1}{6}$

17) $4\frac{3}{8} - 3\frac{1}{6}$

18) $9\frac{3}{5} - 4\frac{5}{6}$

19) $15\frac{14}{15} - 9\frac{3}{4}$

20) $4\frac{2}{13} - 2\frac{1}{4}$

21) $5\frac{1}{9} - 3\frac{3}{8}$

22) $12\frac{1}{2} - 8\frac{1}{3}$

23) $3\frac{9}{10} - 3\frac{1}{5}$

24) $6\frac{2}{3} - 4\frac{7}{12}$

Comparing Fractions

When we compare fractions, it's always easiest when they have a <u>common denominator</u>. Then we can use the inequality symbols < , > , *or* = to compare the fractions.

$\frac{3}{4}$ ■ $\frac{3}{5}$ → Set both to the same denominator → $\frac{15}{20}$ > $\frac{12}{20}$

Compare each pair of fractions using < , > , or =

1) $\frac{19}{9}$ ▢ $\frac{2}{6}$

2) $\frac{5}{9}$ ▢ $\frac{2}{7}$

3) $\frac{6}{9}$ ▢ $\frac{18}{17}$

4) $\frac{3}{7}$ ▢ $\frac{21}{60}$

5) $\frac{5}{9}$ ▢ $\frac{18}{7}$

6) $\frac{19}{2}$ ▢ 8

7) $\frac{13}{3}$ ▢ $\frac{78}{45}$

8) $2\frac{3}{5}$ ▢ $\frac{70}{45}$

9) $\frac{33}{3}$ ▢ $\frac{44}{4}$

10) $\frac{6}{3}$ ▢ $\frac{18}{7}$

11) $\frac{10}{9}$ ▢ $\frac{11}{10}$

12) $\frac{2}{7}$ ▢ $\frac{2}{3}$

13) $\frac{11}{5}$ ▢ $\frac{18}{8}$

14) $\frac{2}{9}$ ▢ $\frac{11}{21}$

15) $\frac{3}{9}$ ▢ $\frac{2}{6}$

16) $\frac{24}{18}$ ▢ $\frac{22}{16}$

17) $\frac{4}{13}$ ▢ $\frac{2}{15}$

18) $\frac{14}{25}$ ▢ $\frac{22}{49}$

19) $\frac{13}{3}$ ▢ $\frac{12}{7}$

20) $\frac{1}{2}$ ▢ $\frac{78}{156}$

21) $\frac{22}{6}$ ▢ $\frac{12}{3}$

22) $\frac{24}{4}$ ▢ $\frac{11}{5}$

23) $\frac{3}{9}$ ▢ $\frac{7}{18}$

24) $\frac{9}{30}$ ▢ $\frac{7}{24}$

25) $\frac{10}{1000}$ ▢ $\frac{2}{200}$

26) $\frac{25}{3}$ ▢ $\frac{25}{4}$

27) $\frac{1}{1000}$ ▢ $\frac{2}{2000}$

28) $\frac{1}{5}$ ▢ $\frac{3}{12}$

29) $\frac{1}{3}$ ▢ $\frac{1}{5}$

30) $\frac{5}{9}$ ▢ $\frac{2}{4}$

31) $\frac{1}{5}$ ▢ $\frac{1}{8}$

32) $\frac{21}{9}$ ▢ $\frac{30}{16}$

33) $\frac{3}{8}$ ▢ $\frac{1}{5}$

34) $\frac{12}{18}$ ▢ $\frac{14}{20}$

35) $4\frac{2}{15}$ ▢ $3\frac{7}{20}$

36) $\frac{18}{5}$ ▢ $\frac{34}{15}$

When adding decimals we need to make sure that:

1. The decimal points line up with each other.

2. Where necessary, put zero placeholders in empty spaces.

3. Drop-down the decimal point.

4. Starting from the far right, add the numbers like regular adddition.

$$\begin{array}{r} 0.73 \\ + \ 0.37 \\ \hline 1.10 \end{array}$$

Add.

1)   .38
   + .14

2)   .85
   + .36

3)   .25
   + .15

4)   .63
   + .12

5)   88
   + .78

6)   .53
   + .20

7)   .99
   + .42

8)   .79
   + .63

9)   .35
   + .21

10)   .53
   + .34

11)   .99
   + .75

12)   .77
   + .14

13)   .53
   + .20

14)   .89
   + .34

15)   .35
   + .19

16)   .33
   + .21

17)   .49
   + .34

18)   .99
   + .69

19)   .78
   + .04

20)   .45
   + .30

21)   .77
   + .69

22)   .33
   + .22

23)   .43
   + .28

24)   .50
   + .40

25)   .92
   + .53

26)   .19
   + .03

27)   .09
   + .01

28)   .51
   + .43

29)   .89
   + .78

30)   .81
   + .44

Score: __/__   Time: __:__

When subtracting decimals we need to make sure that:

1. The decimal points line up with each other.

2. Where necessary, put zero placeholders in empty spaces.

3. Drop-down the decimal point.

4. Starting from the far right, add the numbers like regular addition.

Subtract.

1)   .71
   + .37
   _____

2)   .64
   + .25
   _____

3)   .44
   + .35
   _____

4)   .90
   + .57
   _____

5)   .88
   + .59
   _____

6)   .82
   + .45
   _____

7)   .34
   + .25
   _____

8)   .18
   + .02
   _____

9)   .90
   + .89
   _____

10)   .93
   + .62
   _____

11)   .81
   + .25
   _____

12)   .83
   + .25
   _____

13)   .64
   + .15
   _____

14)   .77
   + .58
   _____

15)   .81
   + .63
   _____

16)   .34
   + .18
   _____

17)   .70
   + .53
   _____

18)   .11
   + .03
   _____

19)   .70
   + .07
   _____

20)   .54
   + .15
   _____

21)   .37
   + .25
   _____

22)   .50
   + .30
   _____

23)   .38
   + .19
   _____

24)   .21
   + .05
   _____

25)   .94
   + .54
   _____

26)   .76
   + .08
   _____

27)   .92
   + .39
   _____

28)   .74
   + .61
   _____

29)   .41
   + .05
   _____

30)   .80
   + .21
   _____

Decimal Subtraction

When subtracting decimals we need to make sure that:

1. The decimal points line up with each other.
2. Where necessary, put zero placeholders in empty spaces.
3. Drop-down the decimal point.
4. Starting from the far right, subtract and borrow when necessary.

$$\begin{array}{r} \overset{1\ \ \ 16}{2.\cancel{6}5} \\ -\ 0.80 \\ \hline 1.85 \end{array}$$

Subtract.

1) 2.38
   − .14
   _____

2) 6.18
   − .12
   _____

3) 1.24
   − .63
   _____

4) 3.65
   − .70
   _____

5) 8.13
   − .56
   _____

6) 5.55
   − .19
   _____

7) 6.85
   − .92
   _____

8) 1.67
   − .84
   _____

9) 7.92
   − .65
   _____

10) 10.19
   −   .41
   _____

11) 1.38
   − .14
   _____

12) 4.52
   − .91
   _____

13) 7.37
   − .96
   _____

14) 4.29
   − .80
   _____

15) 6.01
   − .99
   _____

16) 1.07
   − .96
   _____

17) 7.21
   − .80
   _____

18) 3.33
   − .88
   _____

19) 4.08
   − .04
   _____

20) 3.90
   − .25
   _____

21) 1.89
   − .09
   _____

22) 7.05
   − .70
   _____

23) 8.00
   − .36
   _____

24) 5.43
   − .34
   _____

25) 2.83
   − .35
   _____

26) 9.07
   − .94
   _____

27) 2.92
   − .05
   _____

28) 3.19
   − .38
   _____

29) 4.80
   − .99
   _____

30) 8.57
   − .78
   _____

Decimal Subtraction

When subtracting decimals we need to make sure that:
1. The decimal points line up with each other.
2. Where necessary, put zero placeholders in empty spaces.
3. Drop-down the decimal point.
4. Starting from the far right, subtract and borrow when necessary.

$$\begin{array}{r} \overset{8\quad 13\ 11}{9.41} \\ -\ 2.57 \\ \hline 4.84 \end{array}$$

Subtract.

1) 8.57
  − 6.41

2) 6.72
  − 4.65

3) 4.64
  − 2.02

4) 4.46
  − 4.14

5) 9.33
  − 2.17

6) 7.78
  − 6.43

7) 5.44
  − 1.23

8) 7.18
  − 6.08

9) 6.77
  − 5.65

10) 3.39
  − 0.37

11) 12.73
  − 1.36

12) 4.83
  − 3.58

13) 8.98
  − 6.34

14) 9.73
  − 4.23

15) 6.01
  − 3.39

16) 3.33
  − 2.22

17) 7.70
  − 4.05

18) 7.89
  − 5.90

19) 8.33
  − 2.01

20) 3.78
  − 1.50

21) 1.64
  − 0.09

22) 8.12
  − 7.44

23) 4.33
  − 1.99

24) 7.08
  − 4.40

25) 5.14
  − 3.23

26) 8.38
  − 2.52

27) 6.77
  − 0.95

28) 5.90
  − 3.39

29) 2.03
  − 1.00

30) 6.36
  − 5.98

Decimal Subtraction

When subtracting decimals we need to make sure that:

1. The decimal points line up with each other.

2. Where necessary, put zero placeholders in empty spaces.

3. Drop-down the decimal point.

4. Starting from the far right, subtract and borrow when necessary.

$$
\begin{array}{r}
0.568 \\
-\,0.242 \\
\hline
0.326
\end{array}
$$

Subtract

1)   .724
   − .152

2)   .826
   − .459

3)   .374
   − .146

4)   .146
   − .035

5)   .236
   − .135

6)   .348
   − .125

7)   .548
   − .421

8)   .632
   − .378

9)   .189
   − .006

10)   .365
   − .235

11)   .309
   − .216

12)   .932
   − .239

13)   .700
   − .202

14)   .429
   − .400

15)   .555
   − .111

16)   .996
   − .479

17)   .230
   − .105

18)   .765
   − .567

19)   .321
   − .005

20)   .842
   − .008

21)   .989
   − .436

22)   .456
   − .335

23)   .111
   − .099

24)   .437
   − .409

25)   .500
   − .401

26)   .062
   − .008

27)   .409
   − .060

28)   .876
   − .678

29)   .609
   − .066

30)   .951
   − .119

Day 43 — Decimal Subtraction

Score: __ / __

Time: ___ : ___

When subtracting decimals we need to make sure that:

1. The decimal points line up with each other.

2. Where necessary, put zero placeholders in empty spaces.

3. Drop-down the decimal point.

4. Starting from the far right, subtract and borrow when necessary.

5. When borrowing from a 0, the 0 needs to borrow from the next digit.

$$\begin{array}{r} \overset{\;\;\;9\;\;\;9}{\overset{3\;\;\cancel{10}\;\cancel{10}\;\cancel{10}}{4.0\,0\,0}} \\ -\,3.3\,2\,1 \\ \hline 0.6\,7\,9 \end{array}$$

Subtract

1) 3.819
   − 1.845

2) 6.452
   − 3.125

3) 6.382
   − 6.150

4) 5.891
   − 4.185

5) 9.416
   − 6.782

6) 8.125
   − 6.254

7) 6.004
   − 0.010

8) 9.990
   − 4.440

9) 3.890
   − 2.230

10) 7.52
   − 6.80

11) 8.14
   − 5.12

12) 6.38
   − 4.85

13) 7.50
   − 0.66

14) 6.90
   − 0.58

15) 6.01
   − 3.09

16) 0.152
   − 0.016

17) 2.140
   − 0.080

18) 5.101
   − 2.101

19) 2.819
   − 1.005

20) 2.342
   − 1.950

21) 7.250
   − 4.156

22) 5.392
   − 2.435

23) 9.006
   − 2.701

24) 1.125
   − 0.345

25) 4.444
   − 0.013

26) 9.999
   − 4.444

27) 6.240
   − 3.333

28) 4.000
   − 0.080

29) 8.114
   − 7.120

30) 6.038
   − 4.805

MATHPROJECT
Empowering minds

Decimal Subtraction

When subtracting decimals we need to make sure that:
1. The decimal points line up with each other.
2. Where necessary, put zero placeholders in empty spaces.
3. Drop-down the decimal point.
4. Starting from the far right, subtract and borrow when necessary.

$$
\begin{array}{r}
6\overset{15}{\cancel{6}}.\overset{5\ \ 11}{1\cancel{0}2} \\
-\ 39.402 \\
\hline
26.700
\end{array}
$$

Subtract

1) 62.282 − 6.284

2) 25.611 − 6.125

3) 38.382 − 6.114

4) 15.516 − 6.282

5) 12.627 − 6.143

6) 61.857 − 6.156

7) 34.532 − 3.879

8) 26.153 − 3.282

9) 99.541 − 9.528

10) 68.352 − 5.631

11) 35.345 − 6.658

12) 63.185 − 8.250

13) 80.286 − 6.252

14) 54.285 − 6.252

15) 53.123 − 9.876

16) 29.206 − 6.052

17) 94.380 − 4.502

18) 50.103 − 9.006

19) 42.002 − 2.204

20) 15.681 − 2.195

21) 51.123 − 5.432

22) 50.500 − 4.444

23) 71.020 − 3.743

24) 11.111 − 2.222

25) 33.333 − 9.999

26) 26.053 − 9.702

27) 19.401 − 5.320

28) 98.356 − 9.101

29) 15.450 − 1.638

30) 60.105 − 9.200

Day 45   Decimal Subtraction

When subtracting decimals we need to make sure that:
1. The decimal points line up with each other.
2. Where necessary, put zero placeholders in empty spaces.
3. Drop-down the decimal point.
4. Starting from the far right, subtract and borrow when necessary.

$$
\begin{array}{r}
\scriptstyle 17\ 15\ 10 \\
\scriptstyle 4\ 7\ 5\ 0\ 11 \\
58.611 \\
-18.848 \\
\hline
39.763
\end{array}
$$

Subtract

1) 34.643 − 34.346	**7)** 92.521 − 56.561	**13)** 73.802 − 52.523
2) 63.480 − 61.507	**8)** 30.812 − 5.250	**14)** 88.813 − 60.514
3) 28.512 − 15.352	**9)** 95.621 − 81.921	**15)** 28.813 − 10.014
4) 97.293 − 63.510	**10)** 24.562 − 12.512	**16)** 93.852 − 11.111
5) 63.145 − 20.841	**11)** 63.612 − 23.888	**17)** 38.803 − 10.914
6) 35.511 − 25.513	**12)** 70.631 − 40.562	**18)** 45.003 − 33.014

19) 34.643 − 14.310	**25)** 92.501 − 66.610
20) 63.800 − 34.507	**26)** 49.832 − 35.209
21) 58.572 − 55.052	**27)** 95.021 − 80.901
22) 92.003 − 43.501	**28)** 24.060 − 15.012
23) 62.000 − 54.321	**29)** 73.015 − 29.808
24) 73.510 − 15.003	**30)** 72.333 − 40.444

 MATHPROJECT *Empowering minds*

Decimal Multiplication

Decimal multiplication is a lot like your standard multiplication.

Step 1: Ignoring the decimal points, multiply the numbers as you normally would.

Step 2: Afterwards, count and add the decimal places in the problem.

Step 3: Lastly, starting to the right of the last digit in your answer, place the decimal point with respect to how many you counted in the problem.

$$0.\overset{3}{\overset{2}{1}}5 \leftarrow \text{2 decimal places}$$
$$\times 0.64 \leftarrow \text{2 decimal places}$$
$$0\ 60$$
$$+0\ 9\ 0$$
$$0\ 9\ 60 \leftarrow \text{Move 4 decimal places: 2+2=4}$$

Answer: 0.0960

Multiply.

1) .54 x .63	**6)** .23 x .31	**11)** .42 x .34	**16)** .20 x .92
2) .25 x .15	**7)** .44 x .14	**12)** .25 x .09	**17)** .04 x .66
3) .62 x .35	**8)** .47 x .21	**13)** .06 x .05	**18)** .11 x .41
4) .12 x .52	**9)** .01 x .29	**14)** .43 x .25	**19)** .70 x .06
5) .63 x .12	**10)** .07 x .29	**15)** .92 x .08	**20)** .28 x .28

Decimal Multiplication

$$
\begin{array}{r}
{\scriptstyle 5\ 2} \\
{\scriptstyle 6\ 3} \\
0.984 \leftarrow \text{3 decimal places} \\
\times\, 0.078 \leftarrow \text{3 decimal places} \\
\hline
7\,872 \\
+\,068\,88 \\
\hline
0.0767252 \leftarrow \text{Move 6 decimal places:} \\
3 + 3 = 6
\end{array}
$$

Answer: 0.076752

Multiply.

1) .455
x .049

5) .964
x .064

9) .547
x .025

13) .507
x .005

17) .044
x .120

2) .898
x .055

6) .199
x .087

10) .659
x .059

14) .039
x .109

18) .611
x .789

3) .462
x .125

7) .814
x .066

11) .123
x .321

15) .145
x .201

19) .003
x .908

4) .484
x .048

8) .576
x .076

12) .601
x .012

16) .222
x .333

20) .921
x .129

MATHPROJECT
Empowering minds

Decimal Multiplication

$$3.412 \leftarrow \text{3 decimal places}$$
$$+$$
$$\times .012 \leftarrow \text{3 decimal places}$$
$$6824$$
$$+ 3412$$

Zero place holders $\rightarrow$ 0.040944 $\leftarrow$ Move 6 decimal places

Multiply.

1) 3.400
   x .631

5) 5.645
   x .153

9) 6.812
   x .250

13) 6.515
   x .153

17) 1.630
   x .301

2) 1.415
   x .283

6) 8.530
   x .146

10) 3.369
   x .661

14) 3.629
   x .302

18) 4.123
   x .261

3) 1.635
   x .632

7) 6.532
   x .881

11) 7.625
   x .569

15) 2.452
   x .472

19) 9.103
   x .033

4) 3.041
   x .562

8) 6.518
   x .360

12) 3.482
   x .320

16) 4.623
   x .361

20) 4.003
   x .009

Decimal Multiplication

Multiply.

1)
```
    .684
x   .14
_____
   2736
 +6840
0.09576
```

2)
```
    .755
x   .14
_____
```

3)
```
    .487
x   .14
_____
```

4)
```
    .963
x   .14
_____
```

5)
```
    .767
x   .14
_____
```

6)
```
    .747
x   .14
_____
```

7)
```
    .477
x .064
_____
```

8)
```
    .210
x .035
_____
```

9)
```
    .305
x .035
_____
```

10)
```
    .444
x .075
_____
```

11)
```
    .496
x .047
_____
```

12)
```
    .558
x .036
_____
```

13)
```
    .336
x .012
_____
```

14)
```
    .444
x .063
_____
```

15)
```
    .572
x .022
_____
```

16)
```
    .955
x .074
_____
```

17)
```
    .915
x .12
_____
```

18)
```
    .137
x .74
_____
```

MATHPROJECT
Empowering minds

Decimal Multiplication

$$11.321 \leftarrow \text{3 decimal places}$$
$$+$$
$$\times \underline{2.123} \leftarrow \text{3 decimal places}$$
$$24.034\,483 \leftarrow \text{Move 6 decimal places}$$

Answer: 24.034483

Multiply.

1) 63.462
    x 3.246

2) 35.361
    x 5.572

3) 74.334
    x 6.358

4) 46.631
    x 4.351

5) 15.673
    x 5.446

6) 36.267
    x 8.357

7) 24.254
    x 6.853

8) 25.146
    x 9.996

9) 15.116
    x 6.669

10) 84.246
    x 6.005

11) 26.136
    x 2.247

12) 53.437
    x 3.477

13) 26.265
    x 1.478

14) 38.266
    x 7.588

15) 63.250
    x 2.006

16) 73.146
    x 6.421

Decimal Multiplication

Multiply.

1)   24.462
    x   5.643
    ───────
        7 3 3 8 6
        9 7 8 4 8 0
      1 4 6 7 7 2 0 0
    + 1 2 2 3 1 0 0 0 0
    ───────────────
      1 3 8 . 0 3 9 0 6 6

2)   14.357
    x   8.756

3)   62.246
    x   6.251

4)   61.773
    x   7.357

5)   79.704
    x   1.471

6)   35.355
    x   6.852

7)   25.114
    x   2.361

8)   42.246
    x   5.462

9)   52.463
    x   2.842

10)   57.003
     x   6.468

11)   75.123
     x   1.408

12)   17.243
     x   2.008

13)   70.021
     x   6.109

14)   20.222
     x   3.366

15)   97.013
     x   9.701

MATHPROJECT
Empowering minds

Decimal Multiplication

Multiply.

1)
```
    53.560
  x   .643
  ─────────
    160680
   2142400
 +32136000
 ─────────
  34.439080
```

2)
```
   64.246
 x  8.756
 ────────
```

3)
```
   13.277
 x 6.251
 ────────
```

4)
```
   20.742
 x   .357
 ────────
```

5)
```
   69.442
 x  .471
 ────────
```

6)
```
   62.223
 x  .852
 ────────
```

7)
```
   51.537
 x  .361
 ────────
```

8)
```
   47.975
 x  .462
 ────────
```

9)
```
   48.578
 x  .842
 ────────
```

10)
```
   21.742
 x   .86
 ────────
```

11)
```
   40.154
 x    .11
 ────────
```

12)
```
   37.124
 x    6.2
 ────────
```

13)
```
   81.081
 x 1.234
 ────────
```

14)
```
   59.301
 x  4.08
 ────────
```

15)
```
   62.931
 x 4.368
 ────────
```

16)
```
   62.931
 x  4.68
 ────────
```

Step 1: Start by identifying how many decimal places your answer will have.

Step 2: Ignoring the decimal, multiply as usual.

Step 3: From the right of the last number, move the decimal point to the correct spot.

$0.2 \times 0.2 \times 0.3$

↑   ↑   ↑

1 decimal place each
=> move 3 decimal places in the final answer

$2 \times 2 \times 3$
$= 4 \times 3$
$= 12 \rightarrow 0.012$

Answer: 0.012

Multiply.

1) 0.2×0.3

2) 0.4×0.2

3) 0.03×0.5

4) 0.8×1.0

5) 0.1×0.001

6) $0.1 \times 0.1 \times 0.1$

7) 0.12×0.8

8) 0.2×0.22

9) 0.14×0.7

10) 1.36×0.4

11) $1.6 \times 0.4 \times 0.1$

12) $3.1 \times 2.2 \times 1.3$

13) 7.0×0.2

14) 8.1×8.1

15) 0.01×1.0

MATHPROJECT
Empowering minds

Long Division
3 Digit by 1 Digit - No Remainder

Quotient
Divisor | Dividend
Dividend ÷ Divisor = Quotient

Divisor: The number of pieces we want to break another number up into.

Dividend: A number that is being divided.

Quotient: The number of times the divisor fits into the dividend evenly.

Remainder: The amount left over. It occurs when the divisor doesn't exactly divide the dividend.

Long Division Steps

Step 1 - Divide: How many times does the divisor, 5, go into the first digit of the dividend, 375? If it is 0 times, then look at how many times 5 goes into the first 2 digits of the dividend. 5 goes into 37 at least 7 times.

Step 2: Multiply 5 by 7 to get the number that goes below 37.

Step 3: Subtract 35 from 37.

Step 4: Bring down the next number.

Step 5: Repeat steps 1 - 4 until the remainder is zero or smaller than the divisor.

75 ← Quotient
Divisor → 5)375 ← Dividend
−35↓
25
−25
0 ← Remainder

Divide.

1) 8)216

5) 7)161

9) 5)730

13) 6)744

17) 5)925

2) 3)396

6) 3)639

10) 2)226

14) 3)285

18) 3)936

3) 6)252

7) 8)184

11) 4)192

15) 8)792

19) 2)872

4) 2)136

8) 9)828

12) 4)540

16) 7)385

20) 4)636

Long Division
3 Digit by 2 Digit - No Remainder

Score:
___/___

Time:
___:___

Remember the process:
- ÷ **Divide**
- × **Multiply**
- − **Subtract**
- ↓ **Bring Down**
- **Repeat / Remainder**

$$\begin{array}{r} 73 \\ 12\overline{)876} \\ -84\downarrow \\ \hline 36 \\ -36 \\ \hline 0 \end{array}$$

←12 x 7 = 84

←12 x 3 = 36

Divide.

1) 12)468

2) 21)693

3) 34)884

4) 20)660

5) 41)369

6) 24)792

7) 33)726

8) 43)430

9) 33)825

10) 12)876

11) 11)825

12) 81)972

13) 13)585

14) 55)495

15) 17)816

16) 86)602

17) 62)744

18) 21)189

19) 90)720

20) 77)231

MATHPROJECT
Empowering minds

Remember the process:
- ÷ **Divide**
- × **Multiply**
- − **Subtract**
- ↓ **Bring Down**
- **Repeat / Remainder**

```
      724
4 ⟌ 2896
    − 28↓      ← 4 x 7 = 28
      09
    −  8↓      ← 4 x 2 = 8
      16
    − 16       ← 4 x 4 = 16
       0
```

Divide.

1) 8 ⟌ 2952

5) 2 ⟌ 2216

9) 5 ⟌ 1280

13) 6 ⟌ 5640

17) 3 ⟌ 9630

2) 1 ⟌ 2551

6) 2 ⟌ 1462

10) 7 ⟌ 2499

14) 7 ⟌ 4935

18) 2 ⟌ 2472

3) 3 ⟌ 1263

7) 9 ⟌ 5238

11) 4 ⟌ 3948

15) 6 ⟌ 2472

19) 8 ⟌ 5256

4) 4 ⟌ 3560

8) 5 ⟌ 5235

12) 6 ⟌ 7404

16) 5 ⟌ 9140

20) 2 ⟌ 2022

Long Division
4 Digit by 2 Digit - No Remainder

Remember the process:
- ÷ **Divide**
- × **Multiply**
- − **Subtract**
- ↓ **Bring Down**
- **Repeat / Remainder**

$$
\begin{array}{r}
211 \\
25\overline{)5275} \\
-50\downarrow \quad \leftarrow 25 \times 2 = 5 \\
\hline
27 \\
-25\downarrow \quad \leftarrow 25 \times 1 = 25 \\
\hline
25 \\
-25 \quad \leftarrow 25 \times 1 = 25 \\
\hline
0
\end{array}
$$

Divide.

1) $15\overline{)5475}$

5) $70\overline{)7000}$

9) $31\overline{)2325}$

13) $17\overline{)8041}$

2) $27\overline{)9963}$

6) $42\overline{)5166}$

10) $25\overline{)1125}$

14) $47\overline{)6909}$

3) $10\overline{)4110}$

7) $81\overline{)6561}$

11) $42\overline{)8316}$

15) $11\overline{)1221}$

4) $60\overline{)7500}$

8) $35\overline{)4375}$

12) $22\overline{)4884}$

16) $21\overline{)9324}$

MATHPROJECT
Empowering minds

Remember the process:
- ÷ **Divide**
- × **Multiply**
- − **Subtract**
- ↓ **Bring Down**
- **Repeat / Remainder**

```
        128 R1
    3 ) 385
       - 3↓         ← 3 × 1 = 3
        08
       - 6↓         ← 3 × 2 = 6
         25
       - 24         ← 3 × 8 = 24
          1         ← Remainder = 1
```

Divide.

1) 5)463

2) 9)247

3) 8)455

4) 3)311

5) 5)296

6) 2)466

7) 7)221

8) 5)621

9) 2)223

10) 6)254

11) 2)957

12) 8)500

Long Division
3 Digit by 2 Digit - With Remainder

Score: __ / __

Time: __ : __

Remember the process:
- ÷ **Divide**
- × **Multiply**
- − **Subtract**
- ↓ **Bring Down**
- **Repeat / Remainder**

```
        14 R9
   42 ⟌ 597
      − 42↓      ← 42 × 1 = 42
        177
      − 168      ← 42 × 4 = 168
          9      ← R9
```

Divide.

1) 41 ⟌ 456

2) 25 ⟌ 462

3) 24 ⟌ 369

4) 26 ⟌ 554

5) 25 ⟌ 305

6) 24 ⟌ 774

7) 31 ⟌ 846

8) 12 ⟌ 906

9) 27 ⟌ 490

10) 34 ⟌ 530

11) 29 ⟌ 500

12) 44 ⟌ 908

13) 82 ⟌ 435

14) 66 ⟌ 926

15) 39 ⟌ 145

MATHPROJECT
Empowering minds

Long Division

Day 60

4 Digit by 1 Digit - With Remainder

Score: __/__

Time: ___ : ___

Remember the process:
- ÷ **Divide**
- × **Multiply**
- − **Subtract**
- ↓ **Bring Down**
- **Repeat / Remainder**

Ex 1:

$$\begin{array}{r} 3674 \text{ R1} \\ 2\overline{)7349} \end{array}$$

-6↓ ← 2 x 3 = 6
13
-12↓ ← 2 x 6 = 12
14
-14↓ ← 2 x 7 = 14
09
- 8 ← 2 x 4 = 8
1

Ex 2:

$$\begin{array}{r} 504 \text{ R1} \\ 8\overline{)4033} \end{array}$$

-40↓↓
033
- 32
1

Divide.

1) $4\overline{)5586}$

2) $6\overline{)2475}$

3) $4\overline{)6642}$

4) $8\overline{)8260}$

5) $6\overline{)2208}$

6) $6\overline{)3686}$

7) $3\overline{)3522}$

8) $2\overline{)3350}$

9) $7\overline{)6003}$

10) $9\overline{)1234}$

11) $2\overline{)9837}$

12) $7\overline{)3690}$

13) $3\overline{)9875}$

14) $5\overline{)7539}$

15) $4\overline{)2450}$

16) $9\overline{)7500}$

17) $2\overline{)3897}$

18) $6\overline{)3232}$

19) $7\overline{)3007}$

20) $5\overline{)4321}$

Long Division
4 Digit by 2 Digit - With Remainder

Score: __/__   Time: __:__

Remember the process:
- ÷ **Divide**
- × **Multiply**
- − **Subtract**
- ↓ **Bring Down**
- **Repeat / Remainder**

$$
\begin{array}{r}
174\ R7 \\
35\overline{)6097} \\
-35\downarrow \\
\hline
259 \\
-245\downarrow \\
\hline
147 \\
-140 \\
\hline
7
\end{array}
$$

Divide.

1) 15)5737

4) 24)4969

7) 56)7439

10) 16)5649

13) 81)9039

2) 23)3574

5) 14)4700

8) 27)8546

11) 22)1345

14) 30)3342

3) 25)5835

6) 34)5796

9) 11)6843

12) 99)7649

15) 42)7040

MATHPROJECT
Empowering minds

Decimal Division

Before starting the long division steps, **remember** to place the decimal point in the quotient directly above the decimal point in the dividend. Then follow the same step you did for **long division**.

If necessary, you will write zeros after the last digit in the dividend in order to continue dividing until you reach a remainder of zero **OR** until you reach the necessary decimal places.

```
        3.45
  23) 79.35
     -69 ↓
      103
    - 92 ↓
      115
    - 115
        0
```

Divide to 2 decimal places.

1) 46)13.34   6) 38)34.96   11) 14)12.60   16) 21)44.50   21) 92)84.64

2) 75)23.25   7) 25)20.75   12) 16)14.08   17) 16)25.44   22) 25)59.75

3) 64)71.04   8) 22)74.80   13) 35)12.25   18) 13)59.28   23) 36)72.36

4) 46)4.14   9) 47)39.95   14) 15)52.05   19) 60)51.00   24) 47)25.85

5) 75)48.75   10) 58)13.34   15) 20)39.4   20) 20)99.80   25) 16)60.64

Decimal Division

Before starting the long division steps, **remember** to place the decimal point in the quotient directly above the decimal point in the dividend. Then follow the same step you did for **long division**.

If necessary, you will write zeros after the last digit in the dividend in order to continue dividing until you reach a remainder of zero **OR** until you reach the necessary decimal places.

```
       14.1
   3 ) 42.3
      -3 ↓
       12
      -12 ↓
       03
     -  3
        0
```

Divide to 1 decimal place.

1) 6)3.6

2) 2)15.6

3) 6)5.4

4) 5)7.5

5) 4)15.2

6) 3)5.7

7) 4)16.8

8) 8)9.6

9) 2)8.8

10) 6)3.0

11) 6)33.0

12) 7)12.6

13) 9)77.4

14) 4)93.6

15) 3)77.4

16) 8)87.2

17) 7)70.0

18) 2)93.8

19) 5)99.5

20) 4)63.6

21) 6)7.2

22) 3)96.3

23) 9)22.5

24) 4)91.2

25) 3)60.3

Decimal Division

Remember the process:

- Place the decimal point in the quotient.
- Long Division
- If necessary, write zeros after the decimal in the dividend, until you reach remainder 0 or the necessary decimal places.

$$\begin{array}{r} 2.36 \\ 12\overline{)28.32} \\ -24 \downarrow \\ \hline 43 \\ -36 \downarrow \\ \hline 72 \end{array}$$

Divide to 2 decimal places

1) $22\overline{)44.22}$

2) $12\overline{)69.36}$

3) $26\overline{)91.78}$

4) $26\overline{)48.36}$

5) $35\overline{)70.35}$

6) $42\overline{)84.3}$

7) $35\overline{)59.15}$

8) $12\overline{)51.6}$

9) $10\overline{)42.60}$

10) $40\overline{)10.4}$

11) $81\overline{)31.50}$

12) $66\overline{)43.56}$

13) $81\overline{)80.19}$

14) $33\overline{)81.84}$

15) $10\overline{)70.50}$

16) $41\overline{)41.41}$

17) $59\overline{)56.05}$

18) $53\overline{)85.86}$

19) $46\overline{)75.44}$

20) $95\overline{)42.75}$

Decimal Division

Remember the process:

- Place the decimal point in the quotient.
- Long Division
- If necessary, write zeros after the decimal in the dividend, until you reach remainder 0 or the necessary decimal places.

```
        22.33
   25)558.25
      -50↓
        58
      -50↓
        82
      -75↓
        75
      -75
         0
```

Divide to 2 decimal places.

1) $53\overline{)230.20}$

5) $52\overline{)187.72}$

9) $24\overline{)120.00}$

13) $31\overline{)384.54}$

17) $82\overline{)333.74}$

2) $10\overline{)50.00}$

6) $43\overline{)277.35}$

10) $26\overline{)192.14}$

14) $42\overline{)446.88}$

18) $63\overline{)481.95}$

3) $16\overline{)84.32}$

7) $29\overline{)115.71}$

11) $90\overline{)333.9}$

15) $11\overline{)254.10}$

19) $35\overline{)260.05}$

4) $18\overline{)66.42}$

8) $14\overline{)136.92}$

12) $76\overline{)236.92}$

16) $52\overline{)270.4}$

20) $92\overline{)846.40}$

MATHPROJECT
Empowering minds

Decimal Division

A Different Example:

Since 15 is less than 75, we write a 0 in the quotient.
Next, in order to continue dividing, to get the answer to 2 decimal places, we add a 0 to the dividend. This is so that we can bring it down and turn 15 into 150 (because 75 doesn't divide 15). This also allows us to repeat the long division steps because 150 is big enough to be divided by 75

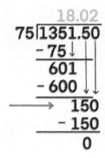

```
           18.02
   75 ) 1351.50
      - 75 ↓
         601
       - 600 ↓↓
    →      150
         - 150
             0
```

Divide to 2 decimal places.

1) 84) 4526.12

5) 76) 3162.67

9) 85) 3620.08

13) 13) 1229.28

2) 25) 4222.39

6) 64) 7840

10) 90) 2620.44

14) 21) 1041.18

3) 33) 3850.88

7) 73) 2716.85

11) 55) 4055.25

15) 30) 8388.60

4) 85) 3840.2

8) 54) 2882.32

12) 38) 2815.8

16) 75) 2407.55

Decimal Division

```
            4.016        Since we know that 4 is not a multiple
    25│100.4             of 25.
     −100 ↓
          40      ←── Put zero till the division is complete
        − 25
         150     ←── Put zero till the division is complete
       − 150
           0
```

Divide to 2 decimal places.

1) 11) 132.02

5) 85) 25.6

9) 86) 314.48

13) 51) 46.41

17) 18) 19.8

2) 84) 160.24

6) 25) 88.40

10) 47) 58.80

14) 9) 467.10

18) 55) 225.5

3) 63) 145.06

7) 48) 190.60

11) 6) 364.2

15) 33) 179.86

19) 2) 170.88

4) 25) 30.2

8) 25) 320.4

12) 80) 63.20

16) 5) 3.25

20) 66) 620.4

MATHPROJECT
Empowering minds

Decimal Operations
Word Problems

Use GRS or GRASS method to answer the word problems.

Questions	Solutions
Eshal's class is planning on taking a trip to the movie theater. Her teacher tells the class that the trip would cost a total of $558.25. How much does each student need to pay if there are 25 students, including Eshal, in the class?	**Given:** Total cost = $558.25, and there are 25 students **Required:** How much does each student pay? **Solution:** Since we need an amount per student, we will divide 558.25 by 25. $$\begin{array}{r} 22.33 \\ 25\overline{)558.25} \\ -50\downarrow \\ \hline 58 \\ -50\downarrow \\ \hline 82 \\ -75\downarrow \\ \hline 75 \\ -75 \\ \hline 0 \end{array}$$ **Therefore, each student needs to pay $22.33.**
1) Jordan works at a coffee shop and gets paid $15.20 per hour. After working for 20 hours, he was paid $325. How much money should Jordan have been paid?	
2) A water tank holds 2205.36 litres of water, and 6 litres of water is drained per day. How many days will it take for the water tank to empty?	
3) Will is fixing the fence around his house. At the store he found out that fencing costs $29.25 per meter. If Will needs to buy 33.66 meters of fencing, how much will it cost him?	

4) Melissa's total grocery bill was $49.44. The cashier gave her $0.58 in change when she paid with a $50 bill.

How much change should the cashier have given Melissa?

5) A 30-foot piece of electrical tape has 6 pieces that are each 3.50 feet cut from it.
What is the new length of the tape?

6) Your new job pays a weekly salary of $1020.00. Your weekly salary needs to cover your weekly spending.

- Rent = $422.80
- Internet = $15.25
- Electricity = $46.38
- Groceries = $180.70

How much do you have left each week after you pay for the following?

7) Ibrahim trained a total of 27.9 hours over the course of 6 days.

On average, how many hours did Ibrahim train per day?

8) Mr.Barley went to the supermarket to buy BBQ sauce. He noticed that they had 2 different bottles, one bottle was 16.9 ounces and the other was 28.32 ounces.

What is the weight difference of the two bottles of BBQ sauce?

Use GRS or GRASS method to answer the word problems.

Questions	Solutions
On Mother's Day, Kamila bought a dozen sunflowers for $28.32. How much did each sunflower cost?	**G:** $28.32 for a dozen (12) **R:** Cost of one sunflower **S:** To find out how much a single sunflower costs we need to divide 28.32 by 12. 2.36 12⟌28.32 − 24 ↓ 43 − 36 ↓ 72 **Therefore, each sunflower cost $2.36.**
1) A movie streaming service charges $12.54 per month. If Sam keeps this membership for 14 months, how much is Sam charged?	
2) The mass of a cup of water is 1.5kg. What is the total mass of 14 cups of water?	
3) Jordan paid $150.80 for 4 books that all cost the same amount. What was the cost per book?	

Use the table below to answer Questions 4 - 7.

Starlight Theater	
Child Ticket : $7.95	Adult Ticket: $13.00
Small Popcorn: $5.50	Large Popcorn: $7.00
Small Drink: $4.00	Large Drink: $5.50
Bag of Candy: $4.20	Nachos: $5.75

4) Find the total cost of three adult tickets, two small drinks and nachos.	
5) Jenna spent $45.70 at the theater. She bought one adult ticket, 2 child tickets and a few bags of candy. How many bags of candy did Jenna buy?	
6) Rhea and her 4 friends decided to buy 3 nachos to share amongst themselves. If they plan to split the cost, how much does each of them need to pay?	
7) Will $ 60 be enough to pay for 2 adult tickets, 3 child tickets, 1 large popcorn, 2 large drinks, and 1 nachos?	

MATHPROJECT
Empowering minds

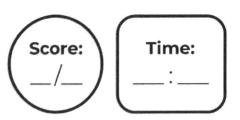

- **Integers** are a set of **whole numbers** and their opposites.

- **Positive integers** are whole numbers **greater than zero.**

- **Negative integers** are whole number **less than zero**

- The **integer 0** is neither positive nor negative.

- Integers have either a **(+) positive** or **(-) negative sign**, except zero, which has no sign.

- A **number line** can be used to represent a set of integers.

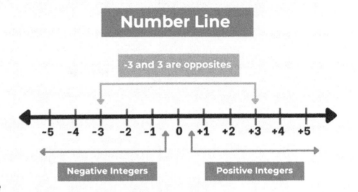

Number Line

-3 and 3 are opposites

-5 -4 -3 -2 -1 0 +1 +2 +3 +4 +5

Negative Integers   Positive Integers

- The **value** of integers **increases** as you move to the **right** along a number line and **decreases** in **value** as you move to the **left**.

A) Write each set of numbers in the correct order from least to greatest.

| **Example:** | -14 | 16 | -13 | -81 | 20 | | -81 | -14 | -13 | 16 | 20 |

1) -16   23   44   -25   78   _____

2) -45   -78   -56   -6   66   _____

3) -2   -74   28   -2   33   _____

4) 7   18   32   -69   4   _____

5) -12   -8   -19   -5   -9   _____

B) Write each set of numbers in the correct order from greatest to least.

Example: 40   -40   -1   0   24 | 40   24   0   -1   -40

1) 56   39   -23   18   -97   _____

2) -41   -26   -1   -45   85   _____

3) 1   50   -15   63   51   _____

4) -10   9   -80   -75   2   _____

5) 70   -7   -3   -34   -6   _____

Score: ___/___   Time: ___ : ___

Addition	Subtraction	Multiplication and Division
Same signs? Keep the sign the same and add the numbers. $$(-5)+(-11) = -16$$ **Different signs?** Take the sign of the greater value and subtract the smaller value from the larger one. $$5 + (-10) = -5$$	An easy way to subtract integers is to change it into an addition statement. **To do this we:** 1) Keep the sign of first number the same. 2) Change the subtraction symbol to addition. 3) Change the sign of the second number to its opposite. This means subtracting a positive integer becomes addition of a negative integer. Then we follow the addition rules: $$(-5) - 10$$ $$= (-5) + (-10)$$ $$= -15$$	Multiply or divide like you normally would. Then determine the correct sign of your answer. **Same signs?** Your answer is positive. $$(-36) \div (-6) = 6$$ **Different signs?** Your answer is negative. $$11 \times (-5) = -55$$

1) $(-63) \div 3 =$

2) $(-9) + 10 =$

3) $-8 - 14 =$

4) $(-7) \times (-4) =$

5) $(-16) - 10 =$

6) $4 - 10 =$

7) $(-52) + 8 =$

8) $6 \times (-8) =$

9) $24 \div (-6) =$

10) $-2 + 4 =$

11) $-18 \div 9 =$

12) $24 + (-19) =$

13) $-19 + (-10) =$

14) $(-15) \div 3 =$

15) $51 - 12 =$

16) $-16 \times 4 =$

17) $-56 \div (-7) =$

18) $14 \times (-5) =$

19) $40 \div (-5) =$

20) $-63 + (-8) =$

21) $-18 - 9 =$

22) $32 \div (-4) =$

23) $24 - 8 =$

24) $13 + (-82) =$

25) $3 - 5 =$

26) $16 - 8 =$

27) $-10 \div 5 =$

28) $-52 - 8 =$

29) $75 \times (-3) =$

30) $42 \times 13 =$

31) $-5 - 7 =$

32) $-54 \div 2 =$

33) $13 - 8 =$

34) $-81 - 25 =$

35) $24 \div (-6) =$

36) $-8 + 23 =$

37) $-36 \div (-6) =$

38) $41 - 21 =$

39) $32 \div (-4) =$

40) $12 - 8 =$

41) $65 + (-9) =$

42) $-44 \div (-11) =$

43) $12 + 82 =$

44) $20 - 53 =$

45) $4 \times (-62) =$

46) $-8 \times (-3) =$

47) $12 \times (-6) =$

48) $-24 \times 5 =$

MATHPROJECT
Empowering minds

Ex. 1: $10 + (-7) = 3$

Ex. 2: $(-24) + (-6) = -30$

Ex. 3: $5 - 25 = -20$

Ex. 4: $10 + 50 = 60$

Ex. 5: $14 - (-36) = 14 + 36 = 50$

Change the subtraction symbol to addition

Then, change the sign of the second number to its opposite.

Evaluate.

1) $42 - (-21) =$

2) $-43 - 42 =$

3) $-13 - 50 =$

4) $31 - 10 =$

5) $-15 - 22 =$

6) $-53 + (-42) =$

7) $24 + (-33) =$

8) $35 + (-54) =$

9) $24 - 52 =$

10) $-54 - 24 =$

11) $14 + (-70) =$

12) $-23 + 12 =$

13) $64 + 32 =$

14) $14 - 41 =$

15) $14 + (-2) =$

16) $32 - 16 =$

17) $-23 - (-22) =$

18) $-45 - (-24) =$

19) $33 - 44 =$

20) $100 + (-100) =$

21) $-21 - 32 =$

22) $9 - 9 =$

23) $28 - (-28) =$

24) $91 - 59 =$

25) $29 - 100 =$

26) $-5 - 42 =$

27) $13 - 4 =$

28) $-100 + (-100) =$

29) $-11 + 62 =$

30) $-1 - 1 =$

31) $54 - (-38) =$

32) $19 - 95 =$

Integer Addition and Subtraction

When adding and subtracting more than one integer it is always best to do it in groups of two, this way you avoid the chance of making a wrong calculation.

For instance the question on the right.

$$-10+30-50$$

First, $-10 + 30$ which is 20.
Then, $20 - 50$ which is -30.

$$= 20-50$$
$$= -30$$

Evaluate.

1) $-5-5 =$

2) $-20-(-40) =$

3) $-20-200 =$

4) $-4-4-4 =$

5) $-9+9-9 =$

6) $60+90-50 =$

7) $-8+(-8)+6 =$

8) $-200-(-200) =$

9) $-80+120 =$

10) $-90+60-20 =$

11) $8-9-12 =$

12) $-30-30+100 =$

13) $-50+50 =$

14) $-30-20-10 =$

15) $20-40 =$

16) $-16+18 =$

17) $1-1+1-1+1 =$

18) $40-80 =$

19) $20-20 =$

20) $-10-10-10 =$

21) $-8+6+6 =$

22) $-80+100 =$

23) $100 - 100 + 200 =$

24) $20-40 =$

MATHPROJECT
Empowering minds

Integer Addition and Subtraction

$$25 - 15 - (-23) \leftarrow \text{Start with } 25 - 15$$
$$= 10 - (-23) \leftarrow \textbf{Two negatives} \text{ make a } \textbf{positive.}$$
$$= 10 + 23$$
$$= 33$$

Evaluate.

1) $31 - 30 + 1 - 1 =$

2) $10 - (-8) - 11 =$

3) $31 - 18 + 8 =$

4) $3 - 6 - (-4) =$

5) $61 - 2 + 60 =$

6) $30 - 24 + 1 =$

7) $6 + (-18) + 16 =$

8) $40 - 39 + 16 =$

9) $11 - 12 + 2 =$

10) $18 - 18 - (-9) - 4 =$

11) $-50 + 9 =$

12) $-12 + 16 =$

13) $6 - (-20) - 28 =$

14) $10 - 6 - 2 - 2 =$

15) $-12 + 4 - 4 + 16 =$

16) $-9 - 9 + 4 =$

17) $-4 - 4 + 8 + 16 =$

18) $-6 - 6 + 12 =$

19) $-4 - 4 - (-8) =$

20) $-14 + 14 - 7 =$

21) $-10 - 9 + 19 =$

22) $-8 - (-16) - 3 + 9 =$

23) $3 - (-12) =$

24) $-52 - (-20) =$

BEDMAS is an acronym that is used to refer to the order of operations.

When evaluating a mathematical expression we have to follow the correct order, otherwise we get the wrong answer.

B	Brackets, ()
E	Exponents, a^n
D M	Division or Multiplication (Left or right)
A S	Addition or Subtraction (Left or right)

$3 \times 6 - (3 \times 6 + 3)$

$= 3 \times 6 - (18 + 3)$

$= 3 \times 6 - (21)$

$= 18 - 21$

$= -3$

HELPFUL TIP: Always do 'division and multiplication' or 'addition and subtraction' from left to right!

Correct:	Incorrect:
$8 - 4 + 2$	$8 - 4 + 2$
$= 4 + 2$	$= 8 - 6$
$= 6$	$= 2$

Solve the following problems using the order of operations.

1) $8 - 4 + 2 + (4 - 5)$

2) $16 - 8 - 8$

3) $(8 - 4) - (4 - 1)$

4) $(5 - 4) - (10 - 5)$

5) $[(20 - 2) - 4]$

6) $(16 + 3) - 18$

7) $(8 \times 8 + 8) - 4$

8) $[(22 - 1) - 19]$

9) $4 - (4 \times 8 + 4)$

MATHPROJECT
Empowering minds

10) $5 \times 6 - 10 + (12 - 6)$

11) $4 \times 4 + 7 - (2 + 3)$

12) $20 - (12 + 10)$

13) $22 - (4 + 10)$

14) $5 \times 5 - 64 \div 8$

15) $30 - (99 \div 3)$

16) $(3 \times 9) - 55 \div 5 - 15$

17) $6 - (6 + 9 - 4)$

18) $(14 + 2) \div (9 - 10)$

19) $33 - (-15 - 20)$

20) $16 - (2 \times (-4))$

21) $-11 \times 4 \div 2 \times 9$

22) $(4 - 10) \times (-9 \div 3)$

23) $28 - (5 \times (-5)) - (-25)$

24) $-11 \times 4 \div (32 \div (-16))$

Order of Operations BEDMAS

( ) { } [ ]	**BRACKETS** - Grouping Symbols	
x^y **or** $\sqrt{x}$	**EXPONENTS** - Powers and Roots	
÷ or x	**DIVISION & MULTIPLICATION**- From left to right	
– or +	**ADDITION & SUBTRACTION** - From left to right	

$$(21 + 69) ÷ [15 \times (2 + 1)]$$
$$= (90) ÷ [15 \times 3]$$
$$= 90 ÷ 45$$
$$= 2$$

Solve the following problems using the order of operations.

1) $[16÷(8÷4)]\times2$

2) $[(24÷3)÷8)]\times14$

3) $[40÷(20÷2)]+12$

4) $[(40÷4÷5)÷2\times10]$

5) $[30-(-30\times20)]+2\times10$

6) $40-(-8-3)$

7) $30\times(-10-10)$

8) $40÷(-45+5)$

9) $-60÷[(10÷(-2)]$

10) $100÷(40÷2)\times10$

11) $(-6)-9-5-(-15)$

12) $(-5)-3-1\times8$

MATHPROJECT
Empowering minds

13) $(21+9) \div 3$

19) $2 \times (-33) - [32 \div (4-8)]$

25) $-2 \times (21-9) + 43$

14) $-40 \times (-4) \times (-2)$

20) $[28 - 13 \times (-6)] + 16$

26) $-80 \times (-20) \div (-2)$

15) $(-20) \times (-20)$

21) $(30-100) \div (-7)$

27) $(-1) \times 24 \div (5-11)$

16) $(-4) \times 20 - 49$

22) $10 \div (-2) + 12 \div 6 \times (-3)$

28) $4 \div 2 - 49 \div (-7)$

17) $(-8) \times [10 - (14 - (-14))]$

23) $[90 \div (30 \div (-10))] \times 5$

29) $[10 - (14 - (-14))] - 10$

18) $50 - [(20-16) - (16-20)]$

24) $-33 + 44 - [22 - 11 \times 3]$

30) $25 + [13 - (26-40)]$

B	Brackets
E	Exponents
D	Division
M	Multiplication
A	Addition
S	Subtraction

$(9 + 5) + (3 - 7 \times 5)$

$= 14 + (3 - 35)$

$= 14 + (-32)$

$= -18$

Solve the following problems using the order of operations.

1) $(8+4) \times 12+4$

2) $(11+40) \div (14+3)$

3) $(12-6)+16 \div 8$

4) $(10+(-12)-4) \div 3$

5) $(14+36) \div (0-25)$

6) $(13+3)+20 \div 2$

7) $(12-3) \times 5-3$

8) $(23+22-6) \div 13$

9) $7 \times 12 \times (12+5)$

10) $6 \times 10 \times (9-12)$

MATHPROJECT
Empowering minds

Order of Operations BEDMAS

Score: __/__

Time: ___:___

| **B**rackets | **E**xponents | **D**ivision | **M**ultiplication | **A**ddition | **S**ubtraction |

Solve the following problems using the order of operations.

1) $(1 \times 12) - (4 \times 4)$

2) $(15 \div 1) + (36 \div 6)$

3) $(63 \div 7) \div 3$

4) $13 \times (2 \div 2)$

5) $(40 \div 2) \div 5$

6) $-15 - (7 - 4)$

7) $(16 - 10) - (-4)$

8) $(3 - 2) \times 13$

9) $8 \times (6 - 4)$

10) $(40 \div 4) \div 5$

11) $6 \times (2 \times 3)$

12) $(20 \div 2) \div 5$

13) $(6 - 1) \times (6 - 2)$

14) $3 \times (6 \times 3)$

15) $6(13 - 3)$

16) $(60 \div 5) \div 4$

17) $(32 \div 4) + (39 \div 3)$

18) $(3 + 2)(0 + 5)$

19) $(10 + 12) \div (4 - 2)$

20) $(3 + 5) \times (14 - 6)$

21) $(80 \div 4) \div 10$

22) $(8 + 19) \div (15 - 12)$

23) $(1 + 35) \div (11 - 5)$

24) $20 \times (-2 - (-5))$

25) $(42 - 57) \times (33 - 30)$

26) $11 \times (66 \div (-3))$

27) $(-16 \div 4) - (8 - 12)$

28) $14 \times 10 \div 20$

29) $-8 \times (3 - 12)$

30) $(39 \div 3) \times (-5)$

Remember

Step 1: Brackets ( )	Solve all problems in parenthesis **first**
Step 2: Exponents 2 , 3 , 4	Next solve any numbers that have exponents
Step 3: Multiply or Divide x , ÷	Then solve any multiplication or division problems (from left to right)
Step 4: Add or Subtract + , −	Finally solve any addiction or subtraction problems (from left to right)

$(-14 \div 2) - (56 \div 8)$
$= (-7) - (7)$
$= -14$

Solve the following problems using the order of operations.

1) $4 \times 8 + 6$

2) $13 + 40 \div 5$

3) $12 \div 4 + 4 \times 3$

4) $3 \times 11 - 15 \div 5$

5) $6 \times 16 \div 6 + 16$

6) $(57 - 18) \div 13 \times 4$

7) $3^2 \times 3$

8) $4^2 \times (14 - 7)$

9) $70 - 4 \times 5$

10) $69 \div 3 - 3 \times 5$

11) $8^2 \div (11 - 7)$

12) $(15 + 15 \div 15) \div (16 - 8)$

13) $-5 \times 12 + (12^2 - 5^2)$

14) $(-20 + 12) - (17 - 3 \times 5)$

15) $18 \div 2 \times 8 + 10 - (-10)$

16) $20 \div (8 - 10)^2$

17) $15 \times (-3) + 9^2$

18) $15 - (-8 \times 10) \div (-4)$

19) $12^2 \div 2^2$

20) $11 \times 12 - (9 - 10)$

21) $25 \times (5) + 2^2$

MATHPROJECT
Empowering minds

Remember

Step 1: Brackets ( )	Solve all problems in parenthesis **first**
Step 2: Exponents 2 , 3 , 4	Next solve any numbers that have exponents
Step 3: Multiply or Divide X , ÷	Then solve any multiplication or division problems (from left to right)
Step 4: Add or Subtract + , −	Finally solve any addition or subtraction problems (from left to right)

Solve the following problems using the order of operations.

1) 24 ÷ 3 + (2 x 8) x 4 + 2

2) 15 – 3 + 8 + 3 x (28 ÷ 4)

3) (18 – 8) x 8 + 5 + 56 – 2

4) 13 – 6 + 6 x 5 + 50 ÷ 5

5) 4 x 5 ÷ (16 + 4) – 45 ÷ 9

6) (24 ÷ 4) ÷ 3 + (10 – 4) x 4

7) 54 ÷ 9 + 24 –10 ÷ 2

8) 9 x 3 + 80 ÷ 8

9) 90 ÷ 15 + (9^2 – 13^2)

10) (9 – 23)² + 78 ÷ 2 (15 – 9)

Solving Simple Binomials
One-Step Equations

Score: __/__

Time: __ : __

One Step Equations & Inverse Operations

When it comes to solving equations the goal is to determine what the value is for the variable (ie. x). In order to solve the equation we need to isolate the variable, which means we need to use inverse (opposite) operations. The reason behind this is that we need to always keep the equation balanced, therefore, what we do to one side we do to the other.

ADDITION	$\longleftrightarrow$	SUBTRACTION	MULTIPLICATION	$\longleftrightarrow$	DIVISION
$x + 7 = 10$ $-7 \quad -7$		$y - 2 = 5$ $+2 \quad +2$	$\dfrac{3a}{3} = \dfrac{-9}{3}$		$2 \times \left(\dfrac{b}{2} \right) = 4 \times 2$
$x = 3$		$y = 7$	$a = -3$		$b = 8$

Solve for the unknown variable.

1) $n + 8 = 5$

2) $36 \div n = 6$

3) $8 \times n = 64$

4) $n - 4 = 10$

5) $n + 16 = 30$

6) $6 + n = 21$

7) $16 \div n = 4$

8) $n \div 13 = 3$

9) $18 - n = 16$

10) $25 \div n = 5$

11) $6 \times g = 24$

12) $8 + k = 1$

13) $-6 \times m = 12$

14) $-8 + k = 1$

15) $n - 18 = 25$

16) $-36 \div n = 6$

17) $2n = 84$

18) $n + 14 = 14$

19) $-5n = 30$

20) $-1 + g = 9$

21) $k \div 8 = -4$

22) $n \div 3 = 33$

23) $8n = 64$

24) $-5 \div n = 5$

25) $-6g = -60$

26) $8 - k = -10$

27) $6m = -24$

28) $18 + k = 6$

29) $n + 8 = -5$

30) $6 \div n = -6$

31) $10n = 80$

32) $n - 25 = -25$

33) $9n = 81$

34) $8 \times g = 800$

35) $k \div 4 = -5$

MATHPROJECT
Empowering minds

Solving Simple Binomials
One-Step Equations

Day 82

Score: __ / __

Time: ___ : ___

$$x - 9 = 15$$
$$+9 \quad +9$$
$$x = 15 + 9$$
$$x = 24$$

$$\frac{3x}{3} = \frac{-30}{3}$$
$$x = \frac{-30}{3}$$
$$x = -10$$

Solve for the unknown variable.

1) $19 - n = 7$

2) $\frac{63}{n} = 9$

3) $n + 15 = 36$

4) $13 - n = 6$

5) $\frac{36}{n} = 3$

6) $n - 13 = 4$

7) $4n = 4$

8) $14 + n = 50$

9) $5 \times n = 30$

10) $n \times 3 = 18$

11) $24 - 15 = n$

12) $5n = 5$

13) $24 - n = 15$

14) $-5n = 100$

15) $1 + n = -17$

16) $\frac{n}{-11} = -9$

17) $n + 25 = 76$

18) $-n = 16$

19) $\frac{100}{n} = -10$

20) $n - (-3) = 4$

21) $-10n = 120$

22) $-9 + n = -10$

23) $-11n = -33$

24) $n \times (-9) = 81$

25) $24 - n = 24$

26) $11n = -11$

27) $15 \div n = -5$

28) $-n = -33$

29) $25 - n = 17$

30) $\frac{-144}{n} = 2$

31) $n - (-5) = 16$

32) $3 - n = -6$

33) $\frac{55}{n} = 11$

34) $n + (-3) = 1$

35) $-10n = -40$

Solving Simple Binomials
One-Step Equations

Score: ___/___

Time: ___ : ___

In this lesson, we teach you algebraic short cuts to solve simple binomials in one step and skip the underlying balancing of equations. This will save you time as you advance to higher grades.

$$\frac{38}{t} = 19$$

switch

$$\frac{38}{19} = t$$

$$2 = t$$

$$12 - m = 40 - 12$$

$$- m = 28$$

$$m = -28$$

Solve for the unknown variable.

1) $8n = 32$

2) $n - 13 = 42$

3) $n \times 11 = 44$

4) $\frac{n}{4} = 16$

5) $n + 6 = 13$

6) $\frac{24}{b} = 4$

7) $n(3) = 21$

8) $18 - n = 14$

9) $n + 17 = 24$

10) $19 + n = 41$

11) $n \times 12 = 96$

12) $\frac{n}{7} = 6$

13) $12 - n = 32$

14) $n + 23 = 43$

15) $-3n = 42$

16) $n - 3 = -2$

17) $n \times 2 = 100$

18) $n \div (-1) = 1$

19) $n + 6 = -12$

20) $4 \div n = -4$

21) $n \times (-3) = -15$

22) $-18 + n = -4$

23) $n - 18 = -41$

24) $-n = 15$

25) $n \times (-2) = 36$

26) $n \div 7 = -11$

27) $-10 - n = 42$

28) $n - 30 = -63$

29) $n \times 8 = -88$

30) $n - 1 = -1$

31) $-11n = -44$

32) $n \div 9 = 9$

33) $n - (-9) = 10$

34) $2 \div n = -1$

35) $3 - n = -21$

MATHPROJECT
Empowering minds

Solving Simple Binomials
One-Step Equations

Score: __/__

Time: __ : __

In this lesson, we teach you algebraic short cuts to solve simple binomials in one step and skip the underlying balancing of equations. This will save you time as you advance to higher grades.

$4 \textcircled{x} e = 44$	Opposite of multiplication is division	$c \textcircled{-} 17 = 20$	Opposite of subtraction is addition
$e = 44 \div 4$		$c = 20 + 17$	
$e = 11$		$c = 37$	

Determine the value of the variable for each equation.

1) $V + 150 = 450$ ★ 300   ★ 600   ★ -300

2) $5n = 25$ ★ -5   ★ 125   ★ 5

3) $e + 632 = 722$ ★ -90   ★ 90   ★ 1354

4) $w - (-27) = 41$ ★ 68   ★ -68   ★ 14

5) $F \div 4 = 21$ ★ 84   ★ -84   ★ 21

6) $y + 52 = -63$ ★ 115   ★ -115   ★ 11

7) $-2C = -122$ ★ -61   ★ 61   ★ 120

8) $H \div 5 = -14$ ★ 70   ★ -70   ★ -9

9) $15z = 225$ ★ 15   ★ 210   ★ -210

10) $L - 16 = -5$ ★ -11   ★ 11   ★ -21

11) $63 \div g = -3$ ★ 21   ★ -189   ★ -21

12) $675 = 15k$ ★ 45   ★ 660   ★ 10 125

13) $B \div 24 = -1$ ★ 24   ★ 1   ★ -24

14) $w - (-9) = 3$ ★ -6   ★ 12   ★ -12

15) $64 \div g = 8$ ★ 8   ★ 512   ★ -8

16) $-v = 30$ ★ 30   ★ 29   ★ -30

Solving Simple Binomials
One-Step Equations

Step 1: Isolate for x by subtracting 9 from both sides.
The opposite of +9 is -9.

You can also think of it as moving it to the other side of the = .
This causes the opposite operation.

$$x + 9 = 3$$
$$- 9 \quad - 9$$
$$x = 3 - 9$$
$$x = - 6$$

Step 2: Simplify/ evaluate the right side to get the final answer.

Solve for the unknown variable.

1) $16 + s = 43$

2) $s - 7 = 18$

3) $22 - s = 42$

4) $s \times 60 = 480$

5) $s \div 6 = 24$

6) $44 - s = 45$

7) $48 \div s = 4$

8) $s \div 12 = 60$

9) $s \div 39 = 3$

10) $s \times 15 = 60$

11) $s + 14 = 23$

12) $23 - s = 23$

13) $22 s = 44$

14) $63 \div s = 3$

15) $10 - s = - 13$

16) $s + 10 = 8$

17) $- m = 42$

18) $s \div 60 = 10$

19) $m \div 6 = - 24$

20) $- 4 - m = 15$

21) $- 4 s = - 4$

22) $s \div (-11) = 6$

23) $s \div 3 = - 22$

24) $m \times 5 = 100$

25) $m + 14 = - 3$

26) $- 11 + m = 23$

27) $-12 s = - 144$

28) $36 \div s = - 3$

MATHPROJECT
Empowering minds

Step 1: Isolate for x by dividing by (-7) from both sides.
   The opposite of x (-7) is ÷ (-7).

You can also think of it as moving it to the other side of the = .
This causes the opposite operation.

$$\frac{-7x}{-7} = \frac{49}{-7}$$

$$\boxed{x = -7}$$

Step 2: Simplify/ evaluate the right side to get the final answer.

Solve for the unknown variable.

1) $\frac{s}{12} = 33$

2) $s \times 16 = 272$

3) $\frac{s}{21} = 13$

4) $9s = 81$

5) $23s = 621$

6) $41s = 492$

7) $\frac{s}{17} = 15$

8) $\frac{899}{s} = 31$

9) $\frac{s}{30} = 2$

10) $\frac{s}{30} = 15$

11) $\frac{s}{26} = 12$

12) $32s = 480$

13) $\frac{s}{14} = 12$

14) $\frac{s}{27} = 1$

15) $\frac{s}{-10} = 5$

16) $S \times 9 = -90$

17) $x \div 11 = 10$

18) $-9s = -180$

19) $3 \times P = 333$

20) $-10m = 490$

21) $-h = 100$

22) $\frac{-21}{s} = 7$

23) $\frac{w}{-3} = -20$

24) $k \div 25 = -5$

25) $\frac{s}{100} = -60$

26) $(-2) \times L = 80$

27) $-a = -55$

28) $\frac{s}{33} = -1$

Step 1: Isolate for x by multiplying by (- 12) to both sides. The opposite of ÷ (-12) is x (-12).

You can also think of it as moving it to the other side of the = . This causes the opposite operation.

$$-12 \times \left(\frac{x}{-12}\right) = 10 \times (-12)$$

$$x = -120$$

Step 2: Simplify/ evaluate the right side to get the final answer.

Solve for the unknown variable.

1) $157\,n = 314$

2) $N \times 18 = 144$

3) $30\,s = 1800$

4) $6\,s = 72$

5) $14s = 224$

6) $\dfrac{112}{s} = 2$

7) $\dfrac{129}{s} = 43$

8) $\dfrac{s}{12} = 14$

9) $s(12) = 144$

10) $s \times 16 = 208$

11) $255 \div s = 15$

12) $s \div 7 = 12$

13) $s \div 12 = 18$

14) $15\,s = 15$

15) $-2\,n = 84$

16) $16\,x = 32$

17) $4\,s = -36$

18) $s \times (-5) = -75$

19) $\dfrac{s}{-9} = -10$

20) $\dfrac{-45}{s} = 3$

21) $22\,p = 462$

22) $\dfrac{s}{14} = -14$

23) $s \times (12) = -144$

24) $\dfrac{s}{8} = 12$

25) $-255 \div s = 5$

26) $s \div (-4) = 55$

27) $m \times 12 = 156$

28) $-15\,s = 15$

MATHPROJECT
Empowering minds

Step 1: Isolate for the unknown fraction by doing the inverse operation to both sides. The opposite of multiplying by $\frac{3}{7}$ is dividing by $\frac{3}{7}$. Divide both sides by $\frac{3}{7}$.

Step 2: Simplify and evaluate the right side to get the unknown fraction. Remember what happens when you divide fractions!

Always cross reduce!

$$\frac{3}{7} \times y = \frac{2}{3}$$

$$\frac{3}{7} \div \frac{3}{7} \times y = \frac{2}{3} \div \frac{3}{7}$$

$$y = \frac{2}{3} \times \frac{7}{3}$$

$$y = \frac{14}{4}$$

Solve for the missing fraction.

1) $\frac{2}{8} \times y = \frac{4}{5}$

5) $\frac{7}{9} \times y = \frac{5}{14}$

9) $\frac{1}{18} \times y = \frac{23}{30}$

2) $\frac{3}{4} \times y = \frac{9}{18}$

6) $\frac{6}{13} \times y = \frac{3}{5}$

10) $\frac{14}{18} \times y = \frac{17}{21}$

3) $\frac{5}{12} \times y = \frac{5}{34}$

7) $\frac{12}{15} \times y = \frac{7}{13}$

11) $\frac{1}{13} \times y = \frac{8}{15}$

4) $\frac{1}{2} \times y = \frac{21}{50}$

8) $\frac{21}{24} \times y = \frac{4}{15}$

12) $\frac{1}{19} \times y = \frac{22}{24}$

Step 1: Turn mixed fractions into improper fractions.

Step 2: Isolate for the unknown fraction by doing the inverse operation to both sides. The opposite of multiplying by 9 is dividing by 9. Divide both sides by 9.

Step 3: Simplify and evaluate the right side to get the unknown fraction. Remember what happens when you divide fractions by whole numbers!

Always cross reduce!

$$9 \times y = 1\frac{3}{5} \quad \text{turn to improper fraction}$$

$$9 \times y = \frac{8}{5}$$

$$9 \div 9 \times y = \frac{8}{5} \div 9$$

$$y = \frac{8}{5} \times \frac{1}{9}$$

$$y = \frac{8}{45}$$

Solve for the missing fraction.

1) $6 \times y = 4\frac{5}{8}$

2) $3 \times y = \frac{3}{4}$

3) $\frac{7}{14} \times y = \frac{6}{12}$

4) $\frac{2}{3} \times y = \frac{4}{9}$

5) $\frac{8}{32} \times y = 3\frac{3}{10}$

6) $\frac{12}{20} \times y = \frac{1}{2}$

7) $7 \times y = \frac{12}{14}$

8) $\frac{1}{16} \times y = 2\frac{1}{10}$

9) $3 \times y = 1\frac{5}{15}$

10) $\frac{6}{15} \times y = \frac{7}{12}$

11) $\frac{4}{9} \times y = \frac{2}{18}$

12) $8 \times y = \frac{18}{20}$

MATHPROJECT
Empowering minds

Solving Equations
Fraction Version

Day 90

Step 1: Isolate for the unknown fraction by doing the inverse operation to both sides. The opposite of multiplying by 1012 is dividing by 1012. Divide both sides by 1012.

Step 2: Simplify and evaluate the right side to get the unknown fraction.

Remember what happens when you divide fractions!

Always cross reduce!

$$\frac{10}{12} \times y = \frac{4}{13}$$

$$\frac{10}{12} \div \frac{10}{12} \times y = \frac{4}{13} \div \frac{10}{12}$$

$$y = \frac{4}{3} \times \frac{12}{10}$$

$$y = \frac{48}{30} = \frac{24}{15}$$

Solve for the missing fraction.

1) $\frac{5}{8} \times y = \frac{7}{17}$

2) $\frac{9}{15} \times y = \frac{45}{81}$

3) $\frac{12}{28} \times y = \frac{14}{60}$

4) $\frac{7}{27} \times y = \frac{9}{42}$

5) $\frac{6}{24} \times y = \frac{6}{10}$

6) $\frac{6}{16} \times y = \frac{1}{30}$

7) $\frac{18}{32} \times y = \frac{8}{36}$

8) $\frac{14}{26} \times y = \frac{7}{13}$

9) $4 \times y = 1\frac{13}{20}$

10) $\frac{9}{16} \times y = \frac{1}{4}$

11) $\frac{5}{7} \times y = \frac{14}{25}$

12) $6 \times y = \frac{1}{36}$

Changing Between Percents and Decimals

Percents ⇒ Decimals	Decimals ⇒ Percents
Step 1: Remove the % sign **Step 2:** Divide by 100 **OR** move the decimal point 2 places to the left. 25% → 25 → 0.25 328% → 328 → 3.28	**Step 1:** Move the decimal point 2 places to the right **OR** multiply by 100 **Step 2:** Add the % sign after the last digit 0.84% → 0.84 → 84% 2.5 → 2.50 → 250%

Part A: Change the following percents into decimals.	Part B: Change the following decimals into percents.
1) 1% =	13) 0.45 =
2) 26% =	14) 0.3 =
3) 46% =	15) 0.12 =
4) 27% =	16) 0.03 =
5) 119 % =	17) 1.03 =
6) 81% =	18) 0.5 =
7) 38% =	19) 0.34 =
8) 46% =	20) 0.65 =
9) 991 % =	21) 4.9 =
10) 55% =	22) 0.11 =
11) 64% =	23) 0.54 =
12) 40% =	24) 9.09 =

Changing Between Percents and Decimals

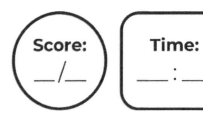
Decimal	Percent
Move decimal 2 places right	

$0.44 \longrightarrow 0.44 \longrightarrow 44\%$

Right

Decimal	Percent
Move decimal 2 places left	

$8\% \longrightarrow 8. \longrightarrow 0.08$

Left

Part A: Change the following percents into decimals.

Part B:
Change the following decimals into percents.

1)	14% =	13)	0.35 =
2)	335 % =	14)	0.5 =
3)	53% =	15)	2.03 =
4)	75% =	16)	0.12 =
5)	50% =	17)	0.42 =
6)	11% =	18)	0.46 =
7)	4% =	19)	0.75 =
8)	25% =	20)	0.24 =
9)	44% =	21)	2.22 =
10)	56% =	22)	9.9 =
11)	63% =	23)	0.45 =
12)	70% =	24)	0.79 =

Percentages of Whole Numbers

Day 93

Score:

___/___

Time:

___:___

When determining the percentage of a whole number there are two methods that can be used.

Method 1: Multiplication	Method 2: Fraction and Division
• Change % into decimal 40% of 120 ↓ ↓ 0.4 x 120 Now, $\begin{array}{r} 120 \\ \times\,0.4 \\ \hline 480 \end{array}$ 1 decimal place **40% of 120 is 48**	• Change % into fraction 40% of 120 ↓ ↓ $\frac{40}{100}$ x 120 Now, $\frac{40}{5\,100}$ x $\frac{120^{6}}{1}$ This is the → same as saying 240 ÷ 5 $= \frac{240}{5}$ $= 48$ **40% of 120 is 48**

Evaluate.

1) 25% x 50

2) 75% x 36

3) 100% x 30

4) 90% x 45

5) 50% x 87

6) 40% x 10

7) 80% x 14

8) 65% x 200

9) 75% x 80

MATHPROJECT
Empowering minds

10) 45% x 120

11) 25% x 48

12) 10% x 30

13) 5% x 48

14) 80% x 20

15) 1% x 24

16) 2% x 23

17) 81% x 12

18) 95% x 2

19) 150% x 10

20) 17% x 17

21) 35% x 20

22) 16% x 42

23) 95 % x 100

24) 50% x 1

25) 41% x 10

26) 64% x 55

27) 50% x 81

Let's practice percentages of whole numbers again.

Determine 46% of 16

Change into a decimal → $\boxed{46\%}$ x 16

= 0.46 x 16

= 7.36

$\overset{2\ 3}{0.46}$ ← 2 decimal places
x 16
———
276
+ 046
———
0736

↖ Move 2 decimal places

Evaluate.

1) 50% x 16

2) 25% x 20

3) 10% x 44

4) 20% x 60

5) 55% x 40

6) 15% x 200

7) 45% x 100

8) 65% x 25

9) 90% x 60

10) 85% x 80

11) 5% x 15

12) 30% x 70

13) 75% x 15

14) 20% x 87

15) 70% x 300

16) 75% x 24

21) 45% x 50

26) 70% x 300

17) 80% x 20

22) 80% x 61

27) 5% x 165

18) 30% x 30

23) 90% x 80

28) 30% x 33

19) 10% x 80

24) 75% x 100

29) 28%x20

20) 80% x 12

25) 20% x 200

30) 9% of 68

120% of 56 ⇒ 1.2 x 56

$$\begin{array}{r} 1.2 \\ \times\ 56 \\ \hline 72 \\ +600 \\ \hline 672 \end{array}$$

1.2 ← 1 decimal place

672 ← **move 1 decimal place**

Therefore, 120% of 56 is **67.2**

Evaluate.

1) 34% of 116

2) 54% of 94

3) 26% of 36

4) 10% of 20

5) 95% of 12

6) 48% of 64

7) 66% of 350

8) 55% of 220

9) 10% of 210

10) 18% of 124

11) 39% of 145

12) 20% of 166

13) 55% of 330

14) 84% of 116

15) 100% of 260

16) 25% of 56

17) 36% of 244

18) 78% of 404

19) 22% of 240

20) 11% of 100

MATHPROJECT
Empowering minds

110 % of 50 ⇒ 1.1 x 50

$$\begin{array}{r} 1.1 \\ \times\ \ 50 \\ \hline 550 \end{array}$$

1.1 ← 1 decimal place

550 ← **move 1 decimal place**

Therefore, 110% of 50 is **55**

Evaluate.

1) 120% of 155

2) 120% of 36

3) 140% of 58

4) 200% of 96

5) 180% of 12

6) 114% of 160

7) 25% of 80

8) 86% of 200

9) 150% of 28

10) 140% of 120

11) 86% of 75

12) 25% of 25

13) 75% of 8

14) 150% of 66

15) 120% of 74

16) 120% of 114

17) 120% of 30

18) 110% of 84

19) 136% of 24

20) 300% of 2

Changing Between Percentages, Fractions & Decimals

Percent ⇒ Fraction	Fraction ⇒ Percent
Step 1: Remove the % sign and make the number your numerator. **Step 2:** Use 100 as the denominator. **Step 3:** Reduce the fraction to lowest terms. $$70\% \longrightarrow \frac{70 \div 10}{100 \div 10}$$ $$\frac{7}{10}$$	**Step 1:** Change the fraction so that the denominator is 100. **Step 2:** Remember that what you do to the denominator you do to the numerator too. **Step 3:** Take only the numerator and add the % sign. $$\overset{\times 20}{\frac{3}{5} = \frac{60}{100}}$$ $$\underset{\times 20}{}$$ $$\frac{3}{5} \longrightarrow 60\%$$

Change the percentages into fractions. Reduce your answer.

1) 100% =

2) 2% =

3) 3% =

4) 4% =

5) 20% =

6) 28% =

7) 25% =

8) 22% =

9) 70% =

10) 80% =

11) 250% =

12) 68% =

13) 190% =

14) 44% =

15) 72% =

MATHPROJECT
Empowering minds

Change the fractions into percentages.

1) $\dfrac{1}{2}$

2) $\dfrac{1}{20}$

3) $\dfrac{6}{8}$

4) $\dfrac{1}{4}$

5) $\dfrac{3}{15}$

6) $\dfrac{7}{100}$

7) $\dfrac{49}{50}$

8) $\dfrac{16}{20}$

9) $\dfrac{3}{10}$

10) $\dfrac{4}{25}$

11) $\dfrac{5}{2}$

12) $\dfrac{11}{50}$

Change the percentages into decimals.

1) 50% =

2) 35 % =

3) 20% =

4) 75 % =

5) 100% =

6) 150% =

7) 3% =

8) 1000% =

Change the decimals into percentages.

1) 0.05 =

2) 0.9 =

3) 2.5 =

4) 0.25 =

5) 1.04 =

6) 7.02 =

7) 0.34 =

8) 0.15 =

Percentage Increases & Decreases

To determine the % increase:

Original Amount	% Increase	New Amount
4	250%	14

$$\text{\% increase} = \frac{(\text{New} - \text{Original})}{\text{Original}} \times 100$$

$$\frac{(14 - 4)}{4} \times 100 = 250\%$$

↑ to turn into a percent

Therefore, there was a 250% increase.

To determine the new amount:

Original Amount	% Increase	New Amount
14	20%	16.8

$$\text{\% increase} = \frac{(\text{New} - \text{Original})}{\text{Original}} \times 100$$

$$20\% = \frac{\text{New} - 14}{14} \times 100$$

$$\longrightarrow \text{New} = 14\,(0.2) + 14 = 16.8$$

Therefore, the final amount after the 20% increase is 16.8.

Complete the following table.

Question	Original Amount	% Increase	New amount	Question	Original Amount	% Increase	New Amount
1)	26	75%	45.5	9)	8	20%	9.6
2)	4	20%		10)	36		54
3)	2	50%		11)	4		16
4)	1	90%		12)	30		90
5)	8	1%		13)	120		210
6)	40	2%		14)	20		25
7)	70	100%		15)	100		125
8)	21	60%		16)	150		495

To determine the % increase:

Original Amount	% Decrease	New Amount
10	20%	8

$$\% \text{ decrease} = \frac{(\text{Original} - \text{New})}{\text{Original}} \times 100$$

$$= \frac{(10 - 8)}{10} \times 100 = 20\%$$

↑ to turn into a percent

Therefore, there was a 20% decrease.

To determine the new amount:

Original Amount	% Decrease	New Amount
50	20%	40

$$\% \text{ decrease} = \frac{(\text{Original} - \text{New})}{\text{Original}} \times 100$$

$$\longrightarrow 20\% = \frac{50 - \text{New}}{50} \times 100$$

$$\longrightarrow \text{New} = 50 - 50\,(0.2) = 40$$

Therefore, the final amount after the 20% decrease is 40

Complete the following table.

Question	Original Amount	% Decrease	New amount	Question	Original Amount	% Decrease	New amount
17)	50	20%	40	25)	10	20%	8
18)	36	50%		26)	16		2
19)	15	2%		27)	25		10
20)	10	36%		28)	50		48
21)	75	12%		29)	200		2
22)	80	75%		30)	160		16
23)	60	50%		31)	5		4
24)	44	90%		32)	125		65

Score: __/__

Time: __ : __

Use the GRS / GRASS Method to answer the following word problems.

Questions	Solutions

You need to buy a new laptop for school but you are waiting for it to go on sale on Boxing Day. It is finally Boxing Day and it is on sale for 20%.
 	
If the laptop originally costs $565.99, how much is the final price?
	G: original price = $565.99 and 20% sale
	R: final price = ?
	S: Percent Decrease
	    100 - 20 = 80% of original price
	    $565.99 x 0.8 = $452.792
	Therefore, the final price of the laptop is $452.79.

1) The $250.99 shoes that Seth wanted to purchase were on sale for 15%. What was the final price of the shoes?	
2) O'neal buys a 6 pound steak at a restaurant, but after it is cooked, the steak loses 25% of its original mass. How much mass did the steak have after being cooked?	
3) It's Taco Day at *Crazy Taco*. Normally, tacos cost $6.50. But on taco day, they are 14% off. How much does one taco cost on Taco Day?	

MATHPROJECT
Empowering minds

4) Russel orders two smoothies from a food delivery service for $52.68, but since he has a membership, he gets 8% off his orders.

With his membership, how much does Russel have to pay?

5) Bruce goes to the theater to watch a movie for $23 total. Since it is Tuesday, he gets 45% off.

What did he pay for the tickets

6) My favorite video game is now 25% off the regular price of $64.99.

What did I pay for my video game?

7) Mishal bought sale tickets to Wateropolis Amusement Pack for $34.50 .

If the tickets originally cost $45.99, how much were the tickets on sale for, as a percent?

8) At the neighborhood block party, the local bakery is selling a box of cookies for $11.25.

If the box of cookies are normally sold for $14.80, what is the percent decrease during the block party?

Use the GRS / GRASS Method to answer the following word problems

Questions	Solutions
The grocery bill comes out to $48.57 plus 13% tax. What is the total price of the groceries with tax?	**G:** bill = $48.57 plus 13 % tax **R:** Total price with tax = ? **S:** Price Increase 100 + 13 = 113% of original price $48.57 x 1.13 = $54. 8841 **Therefore, the total price of the groceries with tax is $54.88.**
1) Steph buys a new flat screen television for $3500. But it is coming from overseas, so she needs to pay 35% more than the original price. How much did Steph pay in total?	
2) Gas prices are currently $1.65 but are expected to rise 40% by tomorrow. How much will gas cost tomorrow?	
3) I purchased an e-bike for $1290.00 but was charged an additional 10% for delivery. What is my total price of the e-bike?	

MATHPROJECT
Empowering minds

4) My pants cost $65.90 plus 8% tax. What is my total?

5) Today's lunch came to $16.00 and I left a 10% tip.

How much did I end up paying for lunch?

6) Your new gaming system cost $890.00 plus 13% tax.

How much did your gaming system cost in total?

7) Last month gas prices were 173. 88 cents per liter. Today gas prices are 201.32 cents per liter.

What is the percent increase on gas since last month?

8) The Cinematic Movie Pass now costs $156.15 for a yearly membership. Last year the yearly membership cost $143.89.

What is the percent increase on the yearly membership?

Use the GRS / GRASS Method to answer the following word problems

Questions	Solutions
1) The price of a pair of shoes is $58. If the price is reduced by 23%, how much will the shoes cost?	
2) $\frac{1}{2}$ of 50% is...	
3) In British Columbia, 68% of its population have a driver license. If there are 5 071 000 people in British Columbia, then how many people have a driver license?	
4) If 4% of a shoe's price is $ 20, then what was the original price?	

MATHPROJECT
Empowering minds

5) During a game show, 3 people won while 13 people lost.

The win rate in percent is...

6) Kevin scores 25 points per game and James scores 15% more than Kevin.

How many points does James score per game?

7) What is 235 % of 28 to the nearest whole number?

8) In gym class there are 28 students and 32% of the class wants to play basketball. Four of those who want to play basketball also want to play badminton.

Out of the students that want to play basketball, what is the percentage who want to play badminton too?

9) If 6% of a number is 72, what is the number?

Use the GRS / GRASS Method to answer the following word problems

Questions	Solutions
1) 40% of 40 is...	
2) In a football team of 50 players, 40% of them play defense and 5 of the players on defense are 24 years old. Of the players on defense, the fraction who are 24 is ...	
3) In the MVP nomination, James received 256 votes, Kevin received 180 votes and Steph received 544 votes. If only 70% of those eligible to vote did so, what is the number of people eligible to vote?	
4) Antetta ordered 50 pieces of chicken nuggets costing $1.45 each. If the tax at the final price was 14%, how much did he pay in total?	
5) Ismael determined that 12.5% of the kids in his grade have food allergies. If there are 8 kids with food allergies, how many kids are in his grade?	

MATHPROJECT
Empowering minds

Percentage Word Problems

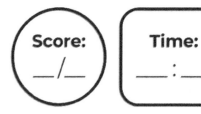

Score:
___/___

Time:
___ : ___

Use the GRS / GRASS Method to answer the following word problems

Questions	Solutions
1) What is the number 50 increased by 150% of itself?	
2) A jacket is on sale for 25% off, if the sale price is $246, what is the original price?	
3) At the pizza place, pizza cost $24. For pizza day, there is a 14% off deal for the pizza. If you bought the pizza at the deal price, how much would it cost including 7% tax?	
4) If P is 25% of Q and Q is 40% of W, find P in terms of W	

5) Determine what $\dfrac{4}{5}$% of 275 is?

6) When you bought your car it cost $8,255. After the first year its value dropped by 15% and then an additional 8% the second year.

How much is your car worth today?

7) A 1925 Peace Silver Dollar coin is worth $128 and it is expected to increase in value every year by 4%.

How much will it be worth in 3 years?

8) A box set of the top five 2020 video games is on sale for 15% off.

If it originally cost $189.90, how much money do you save?

9) Adult movie tickets cost $15.77 and every Tuesday they are 22% off.

If tax is 13%, how much do two adult tickets cost on Tuesday?

Use the GRS / GRASS Method to answer the following word problems

Questions	Solutions
1) A food produce store pays its employees extra based on hours worked in a week. They pay $15/hour for the first 30 hours, then for the next 10 hours they pay $17/hour, then $20/hour for every hour after that. If Eric earns $720 in a week, how many hours did he work?	
2) The area of a rectangle is increased by 20% and the length decreased by 20%. Find the percentage change in the width of the rectangle.	
3) The LA Sparks have a win percentage of 40% of the 50 games played. How many games do they need to win in succession to increase the winning percentage to 50%?	

4) In a recent survey, 60% of gamers play multiplayer. Of those that don't play multiplayer, only 15% are males.

If 250 gamers were surveyed, how many were female and didn't play multiplayer?

5) 200 is reduced by 40%. In order to restore it back to 200, what is the percentage increase needed?

Exponents

What are exponents?

An exponent is a small number that is written to the upper-right of a base number.

Exponents are used to show <u>repeated</u> <u>multiplication</u> of a specific number. It tells us how many times the base number is being multiplied by itself.

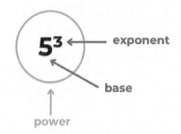

Exponential Form (written as a power)	Word Form	Expanded Form (written as repeated multiplication)	Standard Form (the evaluated answer)
5^3	Five to the power of three	5 x 5 x 5	125

Part A:

Rewrite the following powers using repeated multiplication and calculate its value. For example, $4^3 = 4 \times 4 \times 4 = 64$

1) 5^2

2) 2^5

3) 3^3

4) 7^1

5) 16^2

6) 4^4

Part B:

Rewrite the following expanded forms into exponential form. For example: $5 \times 5 = 5^2$

7) $1 \times 1 \times 1 \times 1 \times 1$

8) 5

9) 2×2

10) 4×4

11) $7 \times 7 \times 7 \times 7 \times 7 \times 7$

12) $8 \times 8 \times 8 \times 8$

Day 106

Reading Exponents

multiply by itself 4 times

$8^4 = 8 \times 8 \times 8 \times 8$

$= 64 \times 64$

$= 4096$

Rewrite the following powers into expanded form and evaluate.

1) 10^4

2) 9^2

3) 2^6

4) 5^3

5) 11^3

6) 4^7

7) 6^3

8) 7^5

9) 3^4

10) 12^3

MATHPROJECT
Empowering minds

Writing Exponents

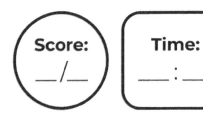

$$4 \times 4 \times 4 \times 4 = 4^{④}$$

Multiply 4 by itself 4 times

Rewrite the following expressions in expanded form into exponent form.

1) $9 \times 9 \times 9$

8) $10 \times 10 \times 10 \times 10 \times 10$

2) 4×4

9) $5 \times 5 \times 5 \times 5 \times 5 \times 5 \times 5$

3) $6 \times 6 \times 6 \times 6$

10) 6

4) $7 \times 7 \times 7$

11) $8 \times 8 \times 8 \times 8 \times 8 \times 8 \times 8$

5) 2×2

12) $5 \times 5 \times 5$

6) $2 \times 2 \times 2 \times 2$

13) $4 \times 4 \times 4 \times 4$

7) 1

14) $6 \times 6 \times 6 \times 6 \times 6 \times 6 \times 6$

Powers of 10

Powers of 10 are used to shrink the size of large numbers into small numbers.

Rather than having multiple zeros, we show how many powers of 10 make that many zeros.

10^0 10^1 10^2 10^3

→

1 10 100 1000

$10^3 = 10 \times 10 \times 10$

$= \underline{1000}$

↑

Since the exponent is 3
there are 3 zeros

Find the value of the following exponents

1) 10^2

2) 10^4

3) 10^1

4) 10^5

5) 10^3

6) 10^9

7) 10^4

8) 10^8

9) 10^6

10) 10^3

11) 10^0

12) 10^7

MATHPROJECT
Empowering minds

Powers of 10

Powers of 10 are used by scientists and engineers to write down larger numbers into smaller numbers. It is commonly referred to as scientific notation.

$$13 \times 10^4 = 13 \times 10000$$
$$= 130000$$

OR

$$13 \times 10^{④}$$
$$= 130000$$

The 13 will be followed by 4 zeros

Find the value of the following exponents.

1) 4×10^3

2) 15×10^4

3) 7×10^5

4) 8×10^6

5) 3×10^2

6) 12×10^8

7) 10×10^2

8) 7×10^1

9) 16×10^4

10) 1×10^3

11) 5×10^3

12) 42×10^0

Powers of 10

$$5000 = 5 \times 1000 \quad \text{3 zeros}$$
$$= 5 \times 10^{3}$$

Rewrite the following numbers using powers of 10.

1) 100000

2) 53

3) 900000

4) 2000000

5) 80

6) 600

7) 34000

8) 5000000000

9) 80000000

10) 2300

11) 30

12) 12000

13) 10

14) 400000

15) 1000000000

16) 7

MATHPROJECT
Empowering minds

Evaluating Exponents

BEDMAS indicates prioritizing operations in the following order:
Brackets, **E**xponents, **D**ivision, **M**ultiplication, **A**ddition and then **S**ubtraction

$5^2 + 2$ ← **Follow BEDMAS rules. Start with the exponent.**

$= 25 + 2$ ← $5^2 = 25$

$= 27$

Evaluate the following exponents.

1) 2^2

2) 2^4

3) 3^3

4) 3^4

5) $4^2 + 10$

6) $5^2 + 8$

7) $6^2 - 4$

8) $8^3 - 6$

9) $81 + 3^2$

10) $6^2 + 2^2$

11) $8^3 + 5^2$

12) $64 + 4^3$

13) $6^2 + 9$

14) $9^2 + 10$

15) $4^2 + 3^2$

16) $3 \times 3 + 3^3$

17) $3^2 + 3^2$

18) $4^2 + 2^2 - 3^3$

19) $4^2 \times 2$

20) $5^2 - 5 + 2^2$

21) $81 - 9^2$

22) $4^2 + 4 - 4^3$

23) 6^3

24) 2×3^2

25) $1 + 6^3 \times 2$

26) $6^2 + 6^3$

27) $3 \times 10^3 - 9^2$

28) $81 - 10^2 \times 4$

29) $2 - 3^2 - 4^3$

30) $4 \times 4^2 + 3^3$

31) 2^6

32) $2^3 - 5^3$

33) $1 \times 2^3 \times 3^2$

34) 22^2

35) $7^2 \div 7$

36) $9^2 \div 3^2$

37) $9 + 9^2$

38) $2^2 + 3^3 \div 9$

39) $11^2 + 12^2$

40) $10^3 \times 2^4$

Perfect Squares & Square Roots

A **perfect square** is a number that is formed by multiplying a whole number by itself.

Did you know that the **square root** of a number is the exact opposite of squaring a number?

The square root of a number is a different number that when multiplied by itself gives the original number.

Essentially, we ask ourselves what number multiplied by itself equals to _____ .

$$\sqrt{4} = 2 \quad 2^2 \text{ or } 2 \times 2 = 4$$

$$\sqrt{9} = 3 \quad 3^2 \text{ or } 3 \times 3 = 9$$

$$\sqrt{16} = 4 \quad 4^2 \text{ or } 4 \times 4 = 16$$

$$\sqrt{25} = 5 \quad 5^2 \text{ or } 5 \times 5 = 25$$

The $\sqrt{}$ symbol is used to evaluate the square root of a number.

For instance:
25 is a perfect square because it is formed by $5 \times 5 = 5^2$.
$\sqrt{25} = 5$ because $5 \times 5 = 25$.

Part A:
Evaluate the following exponents.

1) 2^2

3) $2^2 + 2^3$

5) $3^2 + 2^3$

7) $6^2 + 7$

9) $8^2 - 2^3$

2) 3^2

4) $8^2 + 8$

6) $4^2 + 4^2 - 3^2$

8) $8^2 + 6^2$

10) $2^2 + 6$

Part B:
Evaluate the following square roots.

11) $\sqrt{64}$

13) $\sqrt{25}$

15) $\sqrt{9}$

17) $\sqrt{144}$

19) $\sqrt{10000}$

12) $\sqrt{36}$

14) $\sqrt{49}$

16) $\sqrt{16}$

18) $\sqrt{225}$

20) $\sqrt{121}$

Part C:

Evaluate the following squares.

21) 9^2

22) 13^2

23) 11^2

24) 5^2

25) -15^2

26) 3^2

27) 12^2

28) 8^2

29) 16^2

30) 19^2

31) 21^2

32) 7^2

33) $(-2)^2$

34) 17^2

35) 14^2

36) 20^2

37) 100^2

38) 26^2

39) 30^2

40) $(-5)^2$

41) 21^2

42) 4^2

43) $(-16)^2$

44) 6^2

45) 22^2

46) $(-6)^2$

47) 200^2

48) 15^2

49) -18^2

50) -22^2

Understanding Negative Exponents

What to do when <u>the exponent is negative</u>?

To solve powers that have negative exponents we need to make the exponent positive, this is done by equating it to 1 divided by the number to the positive exponent.

What is happening when we do this is that **we are switching the numerator and denominator.**

$$3^{-3}$$

$$\frac{3^{-3}}{1} = \frac{1}{3^3}$$

$$= \frac{1}{27}$$

- Remember that whole numbers have a denominator of 1

- To Evaluate negative exponents we need to make it positive

- Flip it and make the exponent positive

- Evaluate:
$3^3 = 3 \times 3 \times 3$
$= 27$

Part A:
Rewrite each power so that the exponent is positive.

1) 5^{-1}

3) 4^{-12}

5) 9^{-2}

7) 8^{-1}

9) 2000^{-4}

2) 6^{-4}

4) 10^{-4}

6) 15^{-3}

8) 125^{-5}

10) 13^{-4}

Part B:
Rewrite the following so that the exponent is negative.

11) $\dfrac{1}{5^3}$

13) $\dfrac{1}{10^6}$

15) $\dfrac{1}{12^4}$

17) $\dfrac{1}{25^2}$

19) $\dfrac{1}{100^6}$

12) $\dfrac{1}{6^{14}}$

14) $\dfrac{1}{1^{24}}$

16) $\dfrac{1}{6^{10}}$

18) $\dfrac{1}{10^{14}}$

20) $\dfrac{1}{11^9}$

Evaluating Postive & Negative Exponents

Score: __/__   Time: __:__

$$(-2)^5 = (-2) \times (-2) \times (-2) \times (-2) \times (-2)$$
$$= -32$$

It is negative because the base is negative and the exponent is odd

$$(-2)^4 = (-2) \times (-2) \times (-2) \times (-2)$$
$$= 16$$

It is positive because the base is negative and the exponent is even

$$(-2)^{-5} = \frac{1}{(-2)^5} \leftarrow$$ Make exponent positive, then evaluate

$$= -\frac{1}{32}$$

Evaluate the exponents. Pay attention to the positive and negative exponents.

1) $(-2)^{-6}$

2) 12^{-2}

3) $(-10)^2$

4) 6^0

5) 3^{-2}

6) 4^4

7) 10^{-2}

8) $(-10)^{-2}$

9) $(-3)^{-1}$

10) $(-4)^4$

11) 7^{-1}

12) 4^{-2}

13) $(-3)^{-4}$

14) 12^{-2}

15) 11^{-3}

16) 6^{-3}

17) 8^{-2}

18) $(-9)^3$

19) 6^2

20) 2^{-7}

 MATHPROJECT
Empowering minds

Evaluating Postive & Negative Exponents

$(-3)^3 = (-3) \times (-3) \times (-3)$
$= -27$
↑
It is negative because the base is negative and the exponent is odd

$5^3 = 5 \times 5 \times 5$
$= 25 \times 5$
$= 125$

$5^{-3} = \dfrac{1}{5^3}$
$= \dfrac{1}{125}$

Evaluate the exponents. Pay attention to the positive and negative exponents.

1) $(-5)^{-3}$

2) $(-7)^{-3}$

3) $(-8)^2$

4) $(-3)^4$

5) 2^{-8}

6) 3^3

7) $(-4)^2$

8) $(-10)^{-4}$

9) $(-12)^{-2}$

10) 5^{-4}

11) $(-10)^{-3}$

12) 15^{-2}

13) $(-11)^2$

14) 10^{-1}

15) 9^{-3}

16) $(-6)^3$

17) $(-8)^{-3}$

18) $(-1)^{-5}$

19) $(-2)^{-6}$

20) 11^3

21) $(-3)^{-6}$

Evaluating Postive & Negative Exponents

The same rules/ steps are used when evaluating powers where the base is a fraction.

$$\left(\frac{2}{5}\right)^3 = \frac{2}{5} \times \frac{2}{5} \times \frac{2}{5}$$

$$= \frac{2^3}{5^3}$$

$$= \frac{8}{125}$$

$$\left(\frac{2}{5}\right)^{-3} = \left(\frac{5}{2}\right)^3 \leftarrow$$ Flip the fraction to make the exponent positive then evaluate

$$= \frac{5^3}{2^3}$$

$$= \frac{125}{8}$$

Evaluate the exponents. Remember that all fractions must be reduced.

1) $\left(-\frac{3}{5}\right)^{-4}$

2) $\left(-\frac{4}{5}\right)^{3}$

3) $\left(\frac{2}{3}\right)^{2}$

4) $\left(-\frac{1}{4}\right)^{-5}$

5) $\left(-\frac{1}{4}\right)^{-2}$

6) $\left(-\frac{1}{3}\right)^{4}$

7) $\left(\frac{2}{4}\right)^{-5}$

8) $\left(-\frac{3}{10}\right)^{-7}$

9) $\left(\frac{1}{2}\right)^{-3}$

10) $\left(-\frac{2}{3}\right)^{-3}$

11) $\left(-\frac{2}{3}\right)^{-2}$

12) $\left(-\frac{1}{7}\right)^{-4}$

13) $\left(\frac{1}{4}\right)^{-4}$

14) $\left(-\frac{2}{3}\right)^{-8}$

15) $\left(-\frac{1}{4}\right)^{2}$

16) $\left(-\frac{3}{4}\right)^{-3}$

17) $\left(\frac{3}{8}\right)^{2}$

18) $\left(\frac{4}{5}\right)^{-3}$

19) $\left(\frac{1}{10}\right)^{-4}$

20) $\left(\frac{12}{11}\right)^{-2}$

MATHPROJECT
Empowering minds

Evaluating Postive & Negative Exponents

Step 1: Flip fraction

Step 2: Positive exponent

Step 3: Bring the exponent to the numerator and denominator

Step 4: Evaluate: $10^2 = 10 \times 10 = 100$

$\qquad\quad 7^2 = 7 \times 7 = 49$

$$\left(\frac{7}{10}\right)^{-2} = \left(\frac{10}{7}\right)^{2}$$
$$= \frac{10^2}{7^2}$$
$$= \frac{100}{49}$$

Evaluate the exponents. Remember that all fractions must be reduced.

1) $\left(-\dfrac{1}{12}\right)^{2}$

2) $\left(-\dfrac{5}{9}\right)^{2}$

3) $\left(\dfrac{7}{8}\right)^{-4}$

4) $\left(\dfrac{1}{3}\right)^{-5}$

5) $\left(\dfrac{7}{12}\right)^{3}$

6) $\left(\dfrac{4}{3}\right)^{-3}$

7) $\left(-\dfrac{4}{6}\right)^{8}$

8) $\left(-\dfrac{1}{4}\right)^{2}$

9) $\left(-\dfrac{1}{2}\right)^{4}$

10) $\left(\dfrac{2}{5}\right)^{-2}$

11) $\left(\dfrac{3}{5}\right)^{-2}$

12) $\left(-\dfrac{1}{8}\right)^{-3}$

13) $\left(-\dfrac{6}{10}\right)^{-8}$

14) $\left(-\dfrac{1}{2}\right)^{-2}$

15) $\left(\dfrac{10}{3}\right)^{-3}$

16) $\left(-\dfrac{6}{9}\right)^{-2}$

17) $\left(-\dfrac{1}{2}\right)^{2}$

18) $\left(-\dfrac{2}{3}\right)^{-3}$

19) $\left(-\dfrac{1}{10}\right)^{2}$

20) $\left(\dfrac{6}{7}\right)^{1}$

Ratios and Rates

Ratio	Rate	Unit Rate
A comparison between two or more quantities that have the **same units**. ____ : ____ Reduce the ratio and never write the units.	A comparison between two or more quantities that have **different units**. Reduce the ratio and write the units.	A ratio that compares two different quantities by stating how many of the first quantity compare to **ONE** unit of the second quantity. For instance: 100 km/hour or $12/kg.

Example:
There are 16 boys and 14 girls in the math class.
 	
The ratio would be expressed as
 	
Boys : Girls
  16 : 14 ← **Divide by 2**
   8 : 7 ← **Reduced Ratio**
	Example:
	To get to grandma's house we have to drive 250 km for 3 hours.
	
	The rate would be express as
	
	$\frac{250\ km}{3\ hours}$ **OR** 250 km : 3 hours
		Example:
		Jon paid $45 for 9 hotdogs.
		
		The ratio would be expressed as
		
		$ 45 : 9 Hotdogs ← **Divide by 9**
		$ 5 : 1 Hotdog ← **Reduced Ratio**
		
		The unit rate is $5 per hotdog.

Complete the table by expressing each phrase as a rate and unit rate.

	Phrase	Rate	Unit Rate
1)	21 pineapples for $63		
2)	405 points for 44 games won		
3)	3909 points made over 710 shot attempts		
4)	14 inches of water in 4 hours		
5)	70 miles per hour		
6)	3 monitors cost 240 pesos		
7)	18 phones cost $16400		
8)	$40 for 20 wings		
9)	26 years in prison for 5 banks robbed		
10)	7 pencils for 20 dollars		

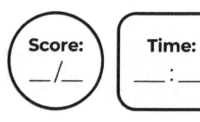

Day 119

Ratios and Rates

Jenny drove 340 km for 4 hours to get to a music concert.	
The rate can be expressed as $\dfrac{340\ km}{4\ hours}$ **OR** *340 km : 4 hours*	The unit rate can be expressed as **340 km : 4 hours** ← **Divide by 4 since we want unit rate** **85 km : 1 hour** ← **Reduce Ratio** **The unit rate is 85 km / hour, which is the speed that Jenny was driving to get to the concert.**

Complete the table by expressing each phrase as a rate and unit rate.

Phrase	Rate	Unit Rate
1) 30 m of fencing for $4600		
2) 6 graphics cards for 580 dollars		
3) 2000 calories burned for 40 km ran		
4) 1400 gallons of water used over 12 days		
5) 15 million tacos made in 4 hours		
6) 81 points in 79 shot attempts		
7) 12 speakers cost $12.00		
8) 1000 miles over 266 seconds		
9) 8 movie tickets cost $22		
10) 5 drinks for a dollar		

Ratios
Word Problems

It's inventory time at your smoothie shop!

Answer the following using ratios.
If needed, round to the nearest hundredth.

Questions	Solution
The ratio of lychee juice bottles to strawberry smoothies is 2:5. If there are 21 lychee juice bottles, how many strawberry smoothies are there?	Lychee : Strawberry $\times \frac{21}{2}$ ($\quad$ **2 : 5** ← Base ratio $\quad$) $\times \frac{21}{2}$ or $\times 10.5$ **21 : X** ← x = # of strawberry smoothies $x = 5 \times \dfrac{21}{2} = 52.5$ **There are 52.5 strawberry smoothies**
1) The ratio of mango bubble tea to Watermelon slush is 3 : 4. If there are 20 mango bubble teas, how many watermelon slush are there?	
2) The ratio of milk teas to matcha teas is 1 : 24. If there are 72 matcha teas, how many milk teas are there?	

MATHPROJECT
Empowering minds

3) The ratio of orange smoothies to peach teas is 6 : 2.

If there are 14 orange smoothies, how many peach teas are there?

4) The ratio of cranberry juice to lemon juice is 12 : 5.

If there are 40 lemon juices, how many cranberry juices are there?

5) There are 36 yogurt smoothies.

If the ratio of yogurt smoothies to grape teas is 4 : 5, how many grape teas are there?

6) There are 25 pina colada smoothies. If the ratio of avocado smoothies to pina colada smoothies is 6 : 10, how many avocado smoothies are there?

Math Fundamentals Answer Key: Day 1-120

Day 1
1. 9/25
2. 5/9
3. 25/64
4. 3/4
5. 160/441
6. 3/5
7. 5/12
8. 16/27
9. 9/32
10. 9/49
11. 20/49
12. 21/80
13. 3/7
14. 45/98
15. 3/16
16. 27/260
17. 11/28
18. 5/6
19. 7/45
20. 1/35
21. 8/45
22. 13/55
23. 13/24
24. 3/14

Day 2
1. 35/16
2. 6/7
3. 8/3
4. 75/8
5. 115/12
6. 9/2
7. 25/2
8. 45/22
9. 19/12
10. 150/17
11. 2
12. 45/2
13. 20/3
14. 16/7
15. 7/2
16. 25/4

Day 3
1. 5/9
2. 2/19
3. 1/18
4. 2/33
5. 3/8
6. 36/125
7. 2/11
8. 5/9
9. 21/110
10. 5/11
11. 3/40
12. 1/27
13. 36/91
14. 13/44
15. 1/8

Day 4
1. 72/25
2. 4/11
3. 160/23
4. 1/80
5. 77/12
6. 1/22
7. 8
8. 1/25
7. 21/2
8. 56/125
9. 77/225
10. 10/49
11. 33/4
12. 1/2
13. 33/4
14. 1/2

Day 5
1. 1/12
2. 11/42
3. 9/20
4. 11/108
5. 21/110
6. 4/27
7. 9/14
8. 1/3

9. 2/11
10. 3/44
11. 15/23
12. 13/25

Day 6
1. 14/5
2. 147/13
3. 209/28
4. 575/84
5. 782/105
6. 651/80
7. 169/112
8. 119/90
9. 16/17
10. 54/35
11. 91/9
12. 25/119
13. 23/32
14. 143/80
15. 103/45

Day 7
1. 39/56
2. 49/90
3. 1/2
4. 1/6
5. 4/63
6. 1/5
7. 13/85
8. 5/24
9. 5/152
10. 2/7
11. 20/3
12. 5/2
13. 21/5
14. 99/70

Day 8
1. 9/8
2. 5/14
3. 11/15

4. 3/2
5. 5/24
6. 13/15
7. 9/32
8. 18/65
9. 28/45
10. 7/10
11. 25/12
12. 25/24
13. 2/3
14. 10/13
15. 21/25
16. 5/8
17. 27/26
18. 120/143

Day 9

1. 55/56
2. 25/12
3. 13/66
4. 7/10
5. 3/13
6. 9/26
7. 3/8
8. 10/11
9. 12/7
10. 25/24
11. 35/18
12. 121/144
13. 54/49
14. 64/63
15. 45/44
16. 100/99
17. 20/91
18. 90/121

Day 10

1. 5/2
2. 2
3. 5/16
4. 5/28
5. 3/5
6. 9/8

7. 2/9
8. 8/9
9. 6/5
10. 21/55
11. 11/2
12. 11/2
13. 20/27
14. 8/5
15. 8/11
16. 22/13
17. 21/50
18. 77/115

Day 11

1. 2
2. 5/4
3. 35/11
4. 15/16
5. 32/15
6. 63/50
7. 25/9
8. 40/9
9. 45/8
10. 45/32
11. 25/21
12. 25/12
13. 25/3
14. 5/8
15. 44/9
16. 21/10
17. 5/3
18. 5/3
19. 7/3
20. 4/3
21. 1

Day 12

1. 2/9
2. 5/12
3. 1/35
4. 7/54
5. 4/35
6. 5/56

7. 1/40
8. 1/10
9. 7/26
10. 1/60
11. 1/18
12. 1/45
13. 7/44
14. 5/32
15. 1/15
16. ⅙
17. 2/9
18. 10/99

Day 13

1. 1/32
2. 1/33
3. 1/16
4. 9
5. 35
6. 35/4
7. 1/10
8. 2/15
9. 1/6
10. 2/7
11. 1/21
12. 6
13. 12
14. 10/9
15. 12
16. 72/7
17. 50
18. 99/7
19. 22/5
20. 32/3
21. 25

Day 14

1. 49/80
2. 15/196
3. 9/95
4. 3/11
5. 56/99
6. 408/49

7. 3/34
8. 1/8
9. 15/38
10. 45/182
11. 143/70
12. 25/156
13. 65/6
14. 74/7
15. 65/4

Day 15

1. 7/180
2. 7
3. 215/18
4. 3/4
5. 15/44
6. 104/5
7. 2/81
8. 4/13
9. 10
10. 45/2
11. 4/9
12. 31
13. 284/15
14. 76/15
15. 19

Day 16

1. 160/63
2. 145/18
3. 5/52
4. 39/100
5. 7/34
6. 3/65
7. 5/44
8. 4/13
9. 5/8
10. 25/102
11. 1/13
12. 1/5
13. 4/99
14. 22/57
15. 10/57

16. 7/24
17. 3/26
18. 50/11

Day 17

1. 8/49
2. 5/4
3. 21/400
4. 98/3
5. 5/54
6. 5/33
7. 3/20
8. 5/14
9. 5/14
10. 3/16
11. 1/26
12. 5/48
13. 9/400
14. 1/4
15. 25/36

Day 18

1. 49/102
2. 145/24
3. 63/152
4. 5/6
5. 245/128
6. 16/39
7. 15/34
8. 55/112
9. 105/92
10. 55/42
11. 216/95
12. 33/46
13. 28/51
14. 56/99
15. 145/102

Day 19

1. 13/38
2. 52/69
3. 22/15
4. 154/75

5. 400/63
6. 112/51
7. 85/42
8. 25/48
9. 10/41
10. 30/19
11. 13/30
12. 13/6
13. 38/15
14. 35/26
15. 2/3

Day 20

1. 9/19
2. 20/51
3. 25/62
4. 3
5. 33/160
6. 7/4
7. 54/13
8. 41/11
9. 53/24

Day 21

1. 25/28
2. 75/44
3. 17/10
4. 85/108
5. 78/85
6. 47/45
7. 77/46
8. 65/44
9. 5/3
10. 20/153

Day 22

1. 17/28
2. 145/162
3. 117/77
4. 4/25
5. 3/22
6. 1/12
7. 8

8. 40/3
9. 45/2
10. 5
11. 5/26
12. 40/203
13. 13/18
14. 13/8
15. 56/15

Day 23
Prime numbers are:
87
23
73
43
53
101
61

Day 24
1. 2x5x5=50
2. 2x2x2x2=16
3. 2x5x7=70
4. 2x43=86
5. 3x3x3x3=81
6. 2x2x3x5=60

Day 25
1. 70
2. 30
3. 60
4. 24
5. 24
6. 20
7. 60
8. 150
9. 52
10. 132

Day 26
1. 48
2. 24
3. 96
4. 12
5. 60
6. 112
7. 56
8. 84
9. 840
10. 24

Day 27
1. 1, 2, 7, 14
2. 1, 3, 9, 27
3. 1, 3, 19, 57
4. 1, 2, 4, 8, 11, 22, 44, 88
5. 1, 2, 11, 22
6. 1, 2, 3, 4, 6, 9, 12, 18, 36
7. 1, 2, 4, 5, 10, 20
8. 1, 3, 13, 39
9. 1, 2, 29, 58
10. 1, 3, 7, 9, 21, 63
11. 1, 2, 4, 7, 8, 14, 28, 56
12. 1, 2, 43, 86
13. 1, 5, 25
14. 1, 2, 23, 46

Day 28
1. 4
2. 2
3. 4
4. 5
5. 9
6. 11
7. 2
8. 15
9. 1
10. 16

Day 29
1. 3
2. 6
3. 9
4. 2
5. 2
6. 13
7. 2
8. 10
9. 5
10. 14

Day 30
1. List multiples of each, notice that all have the lowest common multiple of 28
2. List factors of each, notice that all have the greatest common factor of 6
3. List factors of each, notice that all have the greatest common factor of 2
4. List multiples of each, notice that all have the lowest common multiple of 15
5. A Tuesday is a week day meaning that they occur every 7 days. The LCM of 7 and 14 is 14
6. GCF between 9 and 18 is 9

Day 31

1. 3
2. 8 34/35
3. 11 1/20
4. 12 7/30
5. 6
6. 2 5/6
7. 3 13/40
8. 3 13/40
9. 4 17/20
10. 5 13/28
11. 5 41/45
12. 2 5/6.
13. 4 1/2
14. 4 13/36
15. 3 3/14

Day 32

1. 6 5/22
2. 7 7/8
3. 6 3/14
4. 4 1/8
5. 3 1/2
6. 9 3/10
7. 10 2/5
8. 6
9. 4 41/42
10. 4 11/14

Day 33

1. 5 1/30
2. 8 2/15
3. 5 9/20
4. 5 29/56
5. 7 7/18
6. 5 3/14
7. 5 47/51
8. 10 1/18
9. 3 5/12
10. 2 5/8

Day 34

1. 5 5/6
2. 1 7/10
3. 2 1/12
4. 1 69/80
5. 27/80
6. 1 2/5
7. 7 2/3
8. 4/15
9. 8 7/24
10. 3
11. 6 5/9
12. 4 11/56
13. 2 13/33
14. 31/42
15. 1 43/60
16. 7/30
17. 11/16
18. 6 9/35
19. 1 2/55
20. 1/4
21. 4 111/130
22. 1 4/27
23. 5 13/30
24. 23/72

Day 35

1. 1 34/45
2. 1 13/22
3. 1 19/44
4. 2 3/40
5. 6 9/10
6. 2 31/63
7. 2 7/15
8. 1 23/60
9. 2 9/44
10. 2 3/40
11. 6 10/21
12. 1 3/7
13. 1 13/55
14. 2 13/30
15. 5/12

16. 4 7/15
17. 11/40
18. 1 1/4
19. 5 7/12
20. 2 37/110
21. 21/52
22. 5 11/15
23. 57/77
24. 4 5/14

Day 36

1. 8 5/8
2. 1 1/12
3. 1 17/21
4. 3 7/12
5. 1 11/12
6. 4 5/6
7. 4 1/4
8. 7 47/80
9. 4 1/15
10. 7 1/4
11. 3/10
12. 1 1/4
13. 1 19/45
14. 2 1/21
15. 3 30/77
16. 5 11/18
17. 1 5/24
18. 4 23/30
19. 6 11/60
20. 1 47/52
21. 1 53/72
22. 4 1/6
23. 7/10
24. 2 1/12

Day 37

1. $\dfrac{19}{9} > \dfrac{2}{6}$

2. $\dfrac{5}{9} > \dfrac{2}{7}$

3. $\dfrac{6}{9} < \dfrac{18}{17}$

4. $\dfrac{3}{7} > \dfrac{21}{60}$

5. $\dfrac{5}{9} < \dfrac{18}{7}$

6. $\dfrac{19}{2} > 8$

7. $\dfrac{13}{3} > \dfrac{78}{45}$

8. $2\dfrac{3}{5} > \dfrac{70}{45}$

9. $\dfrac{33}{3} = \dfrac{44}{4}$

10. $\dfrac{6}{3} < \dfrac{18}{7}$

11. $\dfrac{10}{9} > \dfrac{11}{10}$

12. $\dfrac{2}{7} < \dfrac{2}{3}$

13. $\dfrac{11}{5} < \dfrac{18}{8}$

14. $\dfrac{2}{9} < \dfrac{11}{21}$

15. $\dfrac{3}{9} = \dfrac{2}{6}$

16. $\dfrac{24}{18} < \dfrac{22}{16}$

17. $\dfrac{4}{13} > \dfrac{2}{15}$

18.
$\dfrac{14}{25} > \dfrac{22}{49}$

19. $\dfrac{13}{3} > \dfrac{12}{7}$

20. $\dfrac{1}{2} = \dfrac{78}{156}$

21. $\dfrac{22}{6} < \dfrac{12}{3}$

22. $\dfrac{24}{4} > \dfrac{11}{5}$

23. $\dfrac{3}{9} < \dfrac{7}{18}$

24. $\dfrac{9}{30} > \dfrac{7}{24}$

25. $\dfrac{10}{1000} = \dfrac{2}{200}$

26. $\dfrac{25}{3} > \dfrac{25}{4}$

27. $\dfrac{1}{1000} = \dfrac{2}{2000}$

28. $\dfrac{1}{5} < \dfrac{3}{12}$

29. $\dfrac{1}{3} > \dfrac{1}{5}$

30. $\dfrac{5}{9} > \dfrac{2}{4}$

31. $\dfrac{1}{5} > \dfrac{1}{8}$

32. $\dfrac{21}{9} > \dfrac{30}{16}$

33. $\dfrac{3}{8} > \dfrac{1}{5}$

34. $\dfrac{12}{18} < \dfrac{14}{20}$

35. $4\dfrac{2}{15} > 3\dfrac{7}{20}$

36. $\dfrac{18}{5} > \dfrac{34}{15}$

Day 38

1. 0.52
2. 1.21
3. 0.4
4. 0.75
5. 1.66
6. 1.73
7. 1.41
8. 1.42
9. 0.56
10. 0.87
11. 1.74
12. 0.91
13. 0.73
14. 1.23
15. 0.54
16. 0.54
17. 0.83
18. 1.68
19. 0.82
20. 0.75
21. 1.46
22. 0.55
23. 0.71
24. 0.9
25. 1.45
26. 0.22
27. 0.1
28. 0.94
29. 1.67
30. 1.25

Day 39

1. 1.08

2. 0.89
3. 0.79
4. 1.47
5. 1.47
6. 1.27
7. 0.59
8. 0.2
9. 1.79
10. 1.55
11. 1.06
12. 1.08
13. 0.79
14. 1.35
15. 1.44
16. 0.52
17. 1.23
18. 0.14
19. 0.77
20. 0.69
21. 0.62
22. 0.8
23. 0.57
24. 0.26
25. 1.48
26. 0.84
27. 1.31
28. 1.35
29. 0.46
30. 1.01

Day 40

1. 2.24
2. 6.06
3. 0.61
4. 2.95
5. 7.57
6. 5.36
7. 5.93
8. 0.83
9. 7.27
10. 9.78
11. 1.24

12. 3.61
13. 6.41
14. 3.49
15. 5.02
16. 0.11
17. 6.41
18. 2.45
19. 4.04
20. 3.65
21. 1.8
22. 6.35
23. 7.64
24. 5.09
25. 2.48
26. 8.13
27. 2.87
28. 2.81
29. 3.81
30. 7.79

Day 41

1. 2.16
2. 2.07
3. 2.62
4. 0.32
5. 7.16
6. 1.35
7. 4.21
8. 1.1
9. 1.12
10. 3.02
11. 11.37
12. 1.25
13. 2.64
14. 5.5
15. 2.62
16. 1.11
17. 3.65
18. 1.99
19. 6.32
20. 2.28
21. 1.55

22. 0.68
23. 2.34
24. 2.68
25. 1.91
26. 5.86
27. 5.82
28. 2.51
29. 1.03
30. 0.38

Day 42

1. 0.572
2. 0.367
3. 0.228
4. 0.111
5. 0.101
6. 0.223
7. 0.127
8. 0.254
9. 0.183
10. 0.13
11. 0.093
12. 0.693
13. 0.498
14. 0.029
15. 0.444
16. 0.517
17. 0.125
18. 0.198
19. 0.316
20. 0.834
21. 0.553
22. 0.121
23. 0.012
24. 0.028
25. 0.099
26. 0.054
27. 0.349
28. 0.198
29. 0.543
30. 0.832

Day 43

1. 1.974
2. 3.327
3. 0.232
4. 1.706
5. 2.634
6. 1.871
7. 5.994
8. 5.55
9. 1.66
10. 0.72
11. 3.02
12. 1.53
13. 6.84
14. 6.32
15. 2.92
16. 0.136
17. 2.06
18. 3
19. 1.814
20. 0.392
21. 3.094
22. 2.957
23. 6.305
24. 0.78
25. 4.431
26. 5.555
27. 2.907
28. 3.92
29. 0.994
30. 1.233

Day 44

1. 55.998
2. 19.486
3. 32.268
4. 9.234
5. 6.484
6. 55.701
7. 30.653
8. 22.871
9. 90.013
10. 62.721

11. 28.687
12. 54.935
13. 74.034
14. 48.033
15. 43.247
16. 23.154
17. 89.878
18. 41.097
19. 39.798
20. 13.486
21. 45.691
22. 46.056
23. 67.277
24. 8.889
25. 23.334
26. 16.351
27. 14.081
28. 89.255
29. 13.812
30. 50.905

Day 45

1. 0.297
2. 1.973
3. 13.16
4. 33.783
5. 42.304
6. 9.998
7. 35.96
8. 25.562
9. 13.7
10. 12.05
11. 39.724
12. 30.069
13. 21.279
14. 28.299
15. 18.799
16. 82.741
17. 27.889
18. 11.989
19. 20.333
20. 29.293
21. 3.52

22. 48.502
23. 7.679
24. 58.507
25. 25.891
26. 14.623
27. 14.12
28. 9.048
29. 43.207
30. 31.889

Day 46

1. 0.3402
2. 0.0375
3. 0.217
4. 0.0624
5. 0.0756
6. 0.0713
7. 0.0616
8. 0.0987
9. 0.0029
10. 0.0203
11. 0.1428
12. 0.0225
13. 0.003
14. 0.1075
15. 0.736
16. 0.184
17. 0.0264
18. 0.0451
19. 0.042
20. 0.0784

Day 47

1. 0.022295
2. 0.04939
3. 0.05775
4. 0.023232
5. 0.061696
6. 0.017313
7. 0.053724
8. 0.043776
9. 0.013675
10. 0.038881

11. 0.039483
12. 0.007212
13. 0.002535
14. 0.004251
15. 0.029145
16. 0.073926
17. 0.00528
18. 0.482079
19. 0.002724
20. 0.118809

Day 48

1. 2.1454
2. 0.400445
3. 1.03332
4. 1.709042
5. 0.863685
6. 1.24538
7. 5.754692
8. 2.34648
9. 1.703
10. 2.226909
11. 4.338625
12. 1.11424
13. 0.996795
14. 1.095958
15. 1.157344
16. 1.668903
17. 0.49063
18. 1.076103
19. 0.300399
20. 0.036027

Day 49

1. 0.09576
2. 0.1057
3. 0.06818
4. 0.13482
5. 0.10738
6. 0.10458
7. 0.030528
8. 0.00735
9. 0.010675

10. 0.0333
11. 0.023312
12. 0.020088
13. 0.004032
14. 0.027972
15. 0.012584
16. 0.07067
17. 0.1098
18. 0.10138

Day 50

1. 205.997652
2. 197.031492
3. 472.615572
4. 202.891481
5. 85.355158
6. 303.083319
7. 166.212662
8. 251.359416
9. 100.808604
10. 505.89723
11. 58.727592
12. 185.800449
13. 38.81967
14. 290.362408
15. 126.8795
16. 469.670466

Day 51

1. 138.039066
2. 125.709892
3. 389.099746
4. 454.463961
5. 117.244584
6. 242.25246
7. 59.294154
8. 230.747652
9. 149.099846
10. 368.695404
11. 105.773184
12. 34.623944
13. 427.758289
14. 68.067252

15. 941.123113

Day 52

1. 34.43908
2. 562.537976
3. 82.994527
4. 7.404894
5. 32.707182
6. 53.013996
7. 18.604857
8. 22.16445
9. 40.902676
10. 18.69812
11. 4.41694
12. 230.1688
13. 100.053954
14. 241.94808
15. 274.882608
16. 294.51708

Day 53

1. 0.06
2. 0.08
3. 0.015
4. 0.8
5. 0.0001
6. 0.001
7. 0.096
8. 0.044
9. 0.098
10. 0.544
11. 0.064
12. 8.866
13. 1.4
14. 65.61
15. 0.01

Day 54

1. 27
2. 132
3. 42
4. 68
5. 23

6. 213
7. 23
8. 92
9. 146
10. 113
11. 48
12. 135
13. 124
14. 95
15. 99
16. 55
17. 185
18. 312
19. 436
20. 159

Day 55
1. 39
2. 33
3. 26
4. 33
5. 9
6. 33
7. 22
8. 10
9. 25
10. 73
11. 75
12. 12
13. 45
14. 9
15. 48
16. 7
17. 12
18. 9
19. 8
20. 3

Day 56
1. 369
2. 2551
3. 421
4. 890

5. 1108
6. 731
7. 582
8. 1047
9. 256
10. 357
11. 987
12. 1234
13. 940
14. 705
15. 412
16. 1828
17. 3210
18. 1236
19. 657
20. 1011

Day 57
1. 365
2. 369
3. 411
4. 125
5. 100
6. 123
7. 81
8. 125
9. 75
10. 45
11. 198
12. 222
13. 473
14. 147
15. 111
16. 444

Day 58
1. 92 R3
2. 27 R4
3. 56 R7
4. 103 R2
5. 59 R1
6. 233 R0
7. 31 R4

8. 124 R1
9. 111 R1
10. 42 R2
11. 478 R1
12. 62 R4

Day 59
1. 11 R5
2. 18 R12
3. 15 R9
4. 21 R8
5. 12 R5
6. 32 R6
7. 27 R9
8. 75 R6
9. 18 R4
10. 15 R20
11. 17 R7
12. 20 R28
13. 5 R25
14. 14 R2
15. 3 R28

Day 60
1. 1396 R2
2. 412 R3
3. 1660 R2
4. 1032 R4
5. 368 R0
6. 614 R2
7. 1174 R0
8. 1675 R0
9. 857 R4
10. 137 R1
11. 4198 R1
12. 527 R1
13. 3291 R2
14. 1507 R4
15. 612 R2
16. 833 R3
17. 1948 R1
18. 538 R4
19. 429 R4

20. 864 R1

Day 61
1. 382 R7
2. 155 R9
3. 233 R10
4. 207 R1
5. 335 R10
6. 170 R16
7. 132 R47
8. 316 R14
9. 622 R1
10. 353 R1
11. 61 R3
12. 77 R26
13. 111 R48
14. 111 R12
15. 167 R26

Day 62
1. 0.29
2. 0.31
3. 1.11
4. 0.09
5. 0.65
6. 0.92
7. 0.83
8. 3.4
9. 0.85
10. 0.23
11. 0.90
12. 0.88
13. 0.35
14. 3.47
15. 1.97
16. 2.12
17. 1.59
18. 4.56
19. 0.85
20. 4.99
21. 0.92
22. 2.39
23. 2.01

24. 0.55
25. 3.79

Day 63
1. 0.6
2. 7.8
3. 0.9
4. 1.5
5. 3.8
6. 1.9
7. 4.2
8. 1.2
9. 4.4
10. 0.5
11. 5.5
12. 1.8
13. 8.6
14. 23.4
15. 25.8
16. 10.9
17. 10.0
18. 46.9
19. 19.9
20. 15.9
21. 1.2
22. 32.1
23. 2.5
24. 22.8
25. 20.1

Day 64
1. 2.01
2. 5.78
3. 3.53
4. 1.86
5. 2.01
6. 2.00
7. 1.69
8. 4.30
9. 4.26
10. 0.26
11. 0.38
12. 0.66

13. 0.99
14. 2.48
15. 7.05
16. 1.01
17. 0.95
18. 1.62
19. 1.64
20. 0.45

Day 65
1. 4.34
2. 5.00
3. 5.27
4. 3.96
5. 3.61
6. 6.45
7. 3.99
8. 9.78
9. 5.00
10. 7.39
11. 3.71
12. 3.11
13. 12.40
14. 10.64
15. 23.10
16. 5.20
17. 4.07
18. 7.65
19. 7.43
20. 9.20

Day 66
1. 53.88
2. 168.89
3. 116.69
4. 45.17
5. 41.61
6. 122.50
7. 37.21
8. 53.37
9. 42.58
10. 29.11
11. 73.73

12. 74.10
13. 94.56
14. 49.58
15. 279.62
16. 32.10

Day 67
1. 12.00
2. 1.90
3. 2.30
4. 1.208
5. 0.30
6. 3.54
7. 3.97
8. 12.816
9. 3.65
10. 1.25
11. 60.7
12. 0.79
13. 0.91
14. 51.9
15. 5.45
16. 0.65
17. 1.1
18. 4.1
19. 85.44
20. 9.4

Day 68
1. 15.20 x 20 = $304
2. 2205.36 / 6 = 367.56 days
3. 29.25 x 33.66 = $984.56
4. 50 - 49.44 = $0.56
5. 30 - (6 x 3.5) = 9 feet
6. 1020 - 422.8 - 15.52 - 46.38 - 180.7 = $354.87
7. 27.9/6=4.65 hours per day

8. 28.32-16.9= 11.42

Day 69
1. 12.54x14= $175.56
2. 1.5x14=21kg
3. 150.8/4=$37.7
4. (3x13)+(2x4) + 5.75 = $52.75
5. 45.7-13-(2x 7.95) = $16.8 for bag of candy 16.8 / 4.2 = 4 bags of candy
6. 3x5.75=$17.25 17.25 / 5 = $3.45 per person
7. (2x13)+(3x7.95) + 7 + (2 x 5.50) + 5.75 = $67.85 No $ 60 will not be enough.

Day 70
PART A
1. -25,-16,23,44,78
2. -78,-56,-45,-6, 66
3. -74,-2,-2,28,33
4. -69,4,7,18,32
5. -19,-12,-9,-8,-5
PART B
1. 56,39,18,-23, -97
2. 85,-1,-26,-41, -45
3. 63,51,50,1,-15
4. 9,2,-10,-75,-80
5. 70,-3,-6,-7,-34

Day 71
1. -21
2. 1
3. -22
4. 28
5. -26

6. -6
7. -44
8. -48
9. -4
10. 2
11. -2
12. 5
13. -29
14. -5
15. 39
16. -64
17. 8
18. -70
19. -8
20. -71
21. -27
22. -8
23. 16
24. -69
25. -2
26. 8
27. -2
28. -60
29. -225
30. 546
31. -12
32. -27
33. 5
34. -106
35. -4
36. 15
37. 6
38. 20
39. -8
40. 4
41. 56
42. 4
43. 94
44. -33
45. -248
46. 24
47. -72

48. -120

Day 72

1. 63
2. -85
3. -63
4. 21
5. -37
6. -95
7. -9
8. -19
9. -28
10. -78
11. -56
12. -11
13. 96
14. -27
15. 12
16. 16
17. -1
18. -21
19. -11
20. 0
21. -53
22. 0
23. 56
24. 32
25. -71
26. -47
27. 9
28. - 200
29. 51
30. -2
31. 92
32. -76

Day 73

1. -10
2. 20
3. -220
4. -12
5. -9

6. 100
7. -10
8. 0
9. 40
10. -50
11. -13
12. 40
13. 0
14. -60
15. -20
16. 2
17. 1
18. -40
19. 0
20. -30
21. 4
22. 20
23. 200
24. -20

Day 74

1. 1
2. 7
3. 21
4. 1
5. 119
6. 7
7. 4
8. 17
9. 1
10. 5
11. -41
12. 4
13. -2
14. 0
15. 4
16. -14
17. 16
18. 0
19. 0
20. -7
21. 0

22. 14
23. 15
24. -32

Day 75

1. 5
2. 0
3. 1
4. -4
5. 14
6. 1
7. 68
8. 2
9. -32
10. 26
11. 18
12. -2
13. 8
14. 17
15. -3
16. 1
17. -5
18. -16
19. 68
20. 24
21. -198
22. 18
23. 78
24. 22

Day 76

1. 16
2. 14
3. 16
4. 10
5. 650
6. 51
7. -600
8. -1
9. 12
10. 50
11. -5

12. -16
13. 10
14. -320
15. 400
16. -129
17. 144
18. 42
19. -58
20. 122
21. 10
22. -11
23. - 150
24. 22
25. 19
26. - 800
27. 4
28. 9
29. -28
30. 52

Day 77
1. 148
2. 3
3. 8
4. -2
5. -2
6. 26
7. 42
8. 3
9. 1428
10. -180

Day 78
1. -4
2. 21
3. 3
4. 13
5. 4
6. -18
7. 10
8. 13
9. 16

10. 2
11. 36
12. 2
13. 20
14. 54
15. 60
16. 3
17. 21
18. 25
19. 11
20. 64
21. 2
22. 9
23. 6
24. 60
25. -45
26. - 242
27. 0
28. 7
29. 72
30. -65

Day 79
1. 38
2. 21
3. 15
4. 30
5. 32
6. 12
7. 27
8. 112
9. 50
10. 8
11. 16
12. 2
13. 59
14. -10
15. 92
16. 5
17. 36
18. -5
19. 36

20. 133
21. 129

Day 80
1. 74
2. 41
3. 139
4. 47
5. -4
6. 26
7. 25
8. 37
9. -82
10. 430

Day 81
1. -3
2. 6
3. 8
4. 14
5. 14
6. 15
7. 4
8. 39
9. 2
10. 5
11. 4
12. -7
13. -2
14. 9
15. 43
16. -6
17. 42
18. 0
19. -6
20. 10
21. -32
22. 99
23. 8
24. -1
25. 10
26. 18

27. -4
28. -12
29. -13
30. -1
31. 8
32. 0
33. 9
34. 100
35. -20

Day 82

1. 12
2. 7
3. 21
4. 7
5. 12
6. 17
7. 1
8. 36
9. 6
10. 6
11. 9
12. 1
13. 9
14. -20
15. -18
16. 99
17. 51
18. -16
19. -10
20. 1
21. -12
22. -1
23. 3
24. -9
25. 0
26. -1
27. -3
28. 33
29. 8
30. -72
31. 11
32. 9
33. 5

34. 4
35. 4

Day 83

1. 4
2. 55
3. 4
4. 64
5. 7
6. 6
7. 7
8. 4
9. 7
10. 22
11. 8
12. 42
13. -20
14. 20
15. -14
16. 1
17. 50
18. -1
19. -18
20. -1
21. 5
22. 14
23. -23
24. -15
25. -18
26. -77
27. -52
28. -33
29. -11
30. 0
31. 4
32. 81
33. 1
34. -2
35. 24

Day 84

1. 300
2. 5

3. 90
4. 14
5. 84
6. -115
7. 61
8. -70
9. 15
10. 11
11. -21
12. 45
13. -24
14. -6
15. 8
16. -30

Day 85

1. 27
2. 25
3. -20
4. 8
5. 144
6. -1
7. 12
8. 720
9. 117
10. 4
11. 9
12. 0
13. 2
14. 21
15. 23
16. -2
17. -42
18. 600
19. -144
20. -19
21. 1
22. -66
23. -66
24. 20
25. -17
26. 34
27. 12

28. -12

Day 86

1. 396
2. 17
3. 273
4. 9
5. 27
6. 12
7. 255
8. 29
9. 60
10. 450
11. 312
12. 15
13. 168
14. 27
15. -50
16. -10
17. 110
18. 20
19. 111
20. -49
21. -100
22. -3
23. 60
24. -125
25. -6000
26. -40
27. 55
28. -33

Day 87

1. 2
2. 8
3. 60
4. 12
5. 16
6. 56
7. 3
8. 168
9. 12

10. 13
11. 17
12. 84
13. 216
14. 1
15. -42
16. 2
17. -9
18. 15
19. 90
20. -15
21. 21
22. - 196
23. -12
24. 96
25. -51
26. - 220
27. 13
28. -1

Day 88

1. 16/5
2. 2/3
3. 6/17
4. 21/25
5. 45/98
6. 13/10
7. 35/52
8. 32/105
9. 69/5
10. 51/49
11. 104/15
12. 209/12

Day 89

1. 37/48
2. 1/4
3. 1
4. 2/3
5. 66/5
6. 5/6
7. 6/49

8. 168/5
9. 4/9
10. 35/24
11. 1/4
12. 9/80

Day 90

1. 56/85
2. 25/27
3. 49/90
4. 81/98
5. 12/5
6. 4/45
7. 32/81
8. 1
9. 33/80
10. 4/9
11. 98/125
12. 1/216

Day 91

1. 0.01
2. 0.26
3. 0.46
4. 0.27
5. 1.19
6. 0.81
7. 0.38
8. 0.46
9. 9.91
10. 0.55
11. 0.64
12. 0.4
13. 45%
14. 30%
15. 12%
16. 3%
17. 103%
18. 50%
19. 34%
20. 65%
21. 490%

22. 11%
23. 54%
24. 909%

Day 92

1. 0.14
2. 3.35
3. 0.53
4. 0.75
5. 0.5
6. 0.11
7. 0.04
8. 0.25
9. 0.44
10. 0.56
11. 0.63
12. 0.7
13. 35%
14. 50%
15. 203%
16. 12%
17. 42%
18. 46%
19. 75%
20. 24%
21. 222%
22. 990%
23. 45%
24. 79%

Day 93

1. 12.5
2. 27
3. 30
4. 40.5
5. 43.5
6. 4
7. 11.2
8. 130
9. 60
10. 54
11. 12

12. 3
13. 2.4
14. 16
15. 0.24
16. 0.46
17. 9.72
18. 1.9
19. 15
20. 2.89
21. 7
22. 6.72
23. 95
24. 0.5
25. 4.1
26. 35.2
27. 40.5

Day 94

1. 8
2. 5
3. 4.4
4. 12
5. 22
6. 30
7. 45
8. 16.25
9. 54
10. 68
11. 0.75
12. 21
13. 11.25
14. 17.4
15. 210
16. 18
17. 16
18. 9
19. 8
20. 9.6
21. 22.5
22. 48.8
23. 72
24. 75

25. 40
26. 210
27. 8.25
28. 9.9
29. 5.6
30. 6.12

Day 95

1. 39.44
2. 50.76
3. 9.36
4. 2
5. 11.4
6. 30.72
7. 231
8. 121
9. 21
10. 22.32
11. 56.55
12. 33.2
13. 181.5
14. 97.44
15. 260
16. 14
17. 87.84
18. 315.12
19. 52.8
20. 11

Day 96

1. 186
2. 43.2
3. 81.2
4. 192
5. 21.6
6. 182.4
7. 20
8. 172
9. 42
10. 168
11. 64.5
12. 6.25

13. 6
14. 99
15. 88.8
16. 136.8
17. 36
18. 92.4
19. 32.64
20. 6

Day 97

1. 1
2. 1/50
3. 3/100
4. 1/25
5. 1/5
6. 7/25
7. 1/4
8. 11/50
9. 7/10
10. 4/5
11. 5/2
12. 17/25
13. 19/10
14. 11/25
15. 18/25

1. 50%
2. 5%
3. 75%
4. 25%
5. 20%
6. 7%
7. 98%
8. 80%
9. 30%
10. 16%
11. 250%
12. 22%

1. 0.5
2. 0.35
3. 0.2

4. 0.75
5. 1
6. 1.5
7. 0.03
8. 10

1. 5%
2. 90%
3. 250%
4. 25%
5. 104%
6. 702%
7. 34%
8. 15%

Day 98

1. 45.5
2. 4.8
3. 3
4. 1.9
5. 8.08
6. 40.8
7. 140
8. 33.6
9. 20%
10. 50%
11. 300%
12. 200%
13. 75%
14. 25%
15. 25%
16. 230%
17. 40
18. 18
19. 14.7
20. 6.4
21. 66
22. 20
23. 30
24. 4.4
25. 20%
26. 87.5%

27. 60%
28. 4%
29. 99%
30. 90%
31. 20%
32. 48%

Day 99

1. 250.99x0.85 = $213.34
2. 6x0.75 =4.5lbs
3. 6.5x0.86 = $5.59
4. 52.68x0.92 = $48.47
5. 23x0.55 = $12.65
6. 64.99x0.75 = $48.74
7. 34.5/45.99 = 0.75
   1 - 0.75 ->25% off
8. 11.25/14.8=0.76
   1-0.76 ->24%

Day 100

1. 3500x1.35 = $4725
2. 1.65x1.4 = $2.31
3. 1290x1.10 = $1419
4. 65.90x1.08 = $71.17
5. 16x1.10 = $17.6
6. 890x1.13 = $1005.70
7. 201.32/173.88 = 1.157...
   1.157 - 1-> 15.7%
8. 156.15/143.89 = 1.085...
   1.085 - 1 -> 8.5%

Day 101

1. 58 x 0.77 = $44.66
2. 0.5 x 0.5 = 0.25
3. 0.68 x 5071000 =
   3448280
4. 20 / 0.04 = $500
5. 3 / 16 = 18.75%
6. 25 x 1.15 = 28.75
7. 2.35 x 28 = 65.8
   -> 66

8. 28 x 0.32 = about 9 students
   4/9 -> about 44% want badminton
9. 72/0.06 = 1200

Day 102

1. 0.4 x 40 = 16
2. 40 x 0.4 = 20, so the fraction is 5/20 = 1/4
3. (256+180+544) / 0.7 = 1400
4. (50 x 1.45) x 1.14 = $82.65
5. 8 / 0.125 = 64 kids

Day 103

1. 50 x 2.50 = 125
2. 246 / 0.75 = $328
3. (24 x 0.86) x 1.07 = $22.08
4. (0.25 x 0.4W) = 0.1W
5. 0.008 x 275 = 2.2
6. 8255 x 0.85 x 0.77 = $5402.89
7. 128 x 1.04 x 1.04 x 1.04 = $143.98
8. 189.90 x 0.85 = 161.415
   189.9 - 161.415 = $28.485 ->$28.49
9. 15.77 x 2 = 31.54
   31.54 x 0.78 x 1.13 = 27.799...
   -> $ 27. 80

Day 104

1. (720 = (15 x 30) + (17 x 10) + (20 x 5), so 30+10+5 = 45h
2. (1.2 / 0.8) - 1 = 0.5 =50%
3. They win 20/50 games, for a 50% ratio, it needs to be 30/60, so 10 wins.
4. 250 x 0.4 = 100 don't play multiplayer
   100 x 0.85 = 85 females.
5. 200 x 0.6 = 120
   200 / 120 = 1.66..
   66.67% increase

Day 105

1. 25
2. 32
3. 27
4. 7
5. 256
6. 256
7. 1^5
8. 5^1
9. 2^2
10. 4^2
11. 7^6
12. 8^4

Day 106

1. 10 000
2. 81
3. 64
4. 125
5. 1331
6. 16384
7. 216
8. 16807
9. 81
10. 1728

Day 107

1. 9^3
2. 4^2
3. 6^4
4. 7^3
5. 2^2
6. 2^4
7. 1^1
8. 10^5
9. 5^7
10. 6^1
11. 8^7
12. 5^3
13. 4^4
14. 6^7

Day 108

1. 100
2. 10 000
3. 10
4. 100 000
5. 1000
6. 1 000 000 000
7. 10 000
8. 100 000 000
9. 1 000 000
10. 1000
11. 1
12. 10 000 000

Day 109

1. 4000
2. 150 000
3. 700 000

4. 8 000 000
5. 300
6. 1 200 000 000
7. 1000
8. 70
9. 160 000
10. 1000
11. 5000
12. 42

Day 110

1. 1×10^5
2. 53×10^0
3. 9×10^5
4. 2×10^6
5. 8×10^1
6. 6×10^2
7. 34×10^3
8. 5×10^9
9. 8×10^7
10. 23×10^2
11. 3×10^1
12. 12×10^3
13. 1×10^1
14. 4×10^5
15. 1×10^9
16. 7×10^0

Day 111

1. 4
2. 16
3. 27
4. 81
5. 26
6. 33
7. 32
8. 506
9. 90
10. 40
11. 537
12. 128
13. 45
14. 91

15. 25
16. 36
17. 18
18. -7
19. 32
20. 24
21. 0
22. -44
23. 216
24. 18
25. 433
26. 252
27. 2919
28. - 319
29. -71
30. 91
31. 64
32. - 117
33. 72
34. 484
35. 7
36. 9
37. 90
38. 7
39. 265
40. 16000

Day 112

1. 4
2. 9
3. 12
4. 72
5. 17
6. 23
7. 43
8. 100
9. 56
10. 10
11. 8
12. 6
13. 5
14. 7
15. 3

16. 4
17. 12
18. 15
19. 100
20. 11
21. 81
22. 169
23. 121
24. 25
25. - 225
26. 9
27. 144
28. 64
29. 256
30. 361
31. 441
32. 49
33. 4
34. 289
35. 196
36. 400
37. 10000
38. 676
39. 900
40. 25
41. 441
42. 16
43. 256
44. 36
45. 484
46. 36
47. 40000
48. 225
49. - 324
50. - 484

Day 113

1. $1/5^1$
2. $1/6^4$
3. $1/4^{12}$
4. $1/10^4$
5. $1/9^2$
6. $1/15^3$

7. $1/8^1$
8. $1/125^5$
9. $1/2000^4$
10. $1/13^4$
11. 5^{-3}
12. 6^{-14}
13. 10^{-6}
14. 1^{-24}
15. 12^{-4}
16. 6^{-10}
17. 25^{-2}
18. 10^{-14}
19. 100^{-6}
20. 11^{-9}

Day 114

1. 1/64
2. 1/144
3. 100
4. 1
5. 1/9
6. 256
7. 1/100
8. 1/100
9. -1/3
10. 256
11. 1/7
12. 1/16
13. 1/81
14. 1/144
15. 1/1331
16. 1/216
17. 1/64
18. -729
19. 36
20. 1/128

Day 115

1. - 1/125
2. - 1/343
3. 64
4. 81
5. 1/256

6. 27
7. 16
8. 1/10000
9. 1/144
10. 1/625
11. - 1/1000
12. 1/225
13. 121
14. 1/10
15. 1/729
16. -216
17. - 1/512
18. -1
19. 1/64
20. 1331
21. 1/729

Day 116

1. 625/81
2. - 64/125
3. 4/9
4. - 1024
5. 16
6. 1/81
7. 32
8. -10 000 000/2187
9. 8
10. - 27/8
11. 9/4
12. 2401
13. 256
14. 6561/256
15. 1/16
16. - 64/27
17. 9/64
18. 125/64
19. 10000
20. 121/144

Day 117

1. 1/144
2. 25/81
3. 4096/2401

4. 243
5. 343/1728
6. 27/64
7. 256/6561
8. 1/16
9. 1/16
10. 25/4
11. 25/9
12. -512
13. 390 625/6561
14. 4
15. 27/1000
16. 9/4
17. 1/4
18. -27/8
19. 1/100
20. 6/7

Day 118

Phrase	Rate	Unit Rate
1) 21 pineapples for $63	$\dfrac{\$63}{21\ pineapples}$	$3 per pineapple
2) 405 points for 44 games won	$\dfrac{405\ points}{44\ win}$	9.20 points per win
3) 3909 points made over 710 shot attempts	$\dfrac{3909\ points}{710\ shots}$	5.51 points per shot
4) 14 inches of water in 4 hours	$\dfrac{14\ inches}{4\ hours}$	3.5 inches per hour
5) 70 miles per 2 hour	$\dfrac{70\ miles}{2\ hour}$	35 miles per hour
6) 3 monitors cost 240 pesos	$\dfrac{240\ pesos}{3\ monitors}$	80 pesos per monitor
7) 18 phones cost $16400	$\dfrac{\$16400}{18}$	$911.11 per phone
8) $40 for 20 wings	$\dfrac{\$40}{20\ wings}$	$2 per wing
9) 26 years in prison for 5 banks robbed	$\dfrac{26\ years}{5\ banks}$	5.2 years per robbed bank
10) 7 pencils for 20 dollars	$\dfrac{20\ dollars}{7\ pencils}$	$2.86 per pencil

Day 119

Phrase	Rate	Unit Rate
1) 30 metres offencing for $4600	$\dfrac{\$4600}{30\ metres}$	$153.33 per metre
2) 6 graphics cards for 580 dollars	$\dfrac{\$580}{6\ graphic\ cards}$	$96.67 per graphics card
3) 2000 calories burned for 40 kilometres ran	$\dfrac{2000\ calories}{40\ kilometres}$	50 calories per kilometre
4) 1400 gallons of water used over 12 days	$\dfrac{1400\ gallons}{12\ days}$	116.67 gallons per day

5) 15 million tacos made in 4 hours	$\dfrac{15\ 000\ 000\ tacos}{4\ hours}$	3 750 000 tacos per hour
6) 81 points in 79 shot attempts	$\dfrac{81\ points}{79\ shots}$	1.03 points per shot
7) 12 speakers cost 12 dollars	$\dfrac{\$12}{12\ speakers}$	$1 per speaker
8) 1000 miles over 266 seconds	$\dfrac{1000\ miles}{266\ seconds}$	3.76 miles per second
9) 8 movie tickets cost $22	$\dfrac{\$22}{8\ movie\ tickets}$	$2.75 per ticket
10) 5 drinks for a dollar	$\dfrac{\$1}{5\ drinks}$	$0.2 per drink

Day 120

1. 26.67 watermelon slush
2. 3 milk teas
3. 4.67 peach teas
4. 96 cranberry juices
5. 45 grape teas
6. 15 avocado smoothies

Math Fundamentals: Appendix A

Strategies for Solving Word Problems

Many students find word problems to be overwhelming, confusing and/or complicated because there is a lot of information being thrown at them all at once. But it does not have to be like that! There are many strategies that can help us understand, organize and answer word problems.

Below you will find 4 great techniques and strategies to help you work with word problems!

1. Start by <u>carefully reading</u> the question. When you have read the question, take a highlighter/pencil/pen and <u>circle/underline key words</u> that will help you figure out the answer. This will help you figure out what you have and what you need.
For example: What is the sum of all the factors of 10? With a different color you should circle/underline the following keywords **"<u>sum</u>"** and **"<u>factors of 10</u>"**

2. The "GRASS "Method

When it comes to solving word problems, the examples in this workbook use the GRASS method. The reason we use the GRASS method is because it is a useful strategy that helps us understand what the question is asking and what we need to look for.

G: Given	R: Required	A: Action	S: Solve	S: Statement
Write down what information is given in the question. It helps to underline/circle keywords.	Write down what you need to find/answer. What is missing?	Write down how you will solve the question. Operations? Equations?	Calculate the answer. Calculations. Show all your steps.	State your answer in a full sentence.

Here is an example of how to use this method:
At recess, three children decide to count up how much candies they have all together. Emma has 7, Bucky has 9 and Robin has only 1. How many candies do they have in total?

Next ➡

Given: Write down what you know. Underline keywords.

Emma = 7 candies Bucky = 9 candies Robin = 1 candy

Required: What do we want to find out?

Sum / Total of all candies they have together

Action: Write down how you are going to solve the question.

Add all the candies together.
Emma + Bucky + Robin = Total of Candies

Solution: Solve the question.

Emma + Bucky + Robin = Total of Candies
7+9+1=17

Statement: Write a sentence that answers the question.

In total, they have 17 candies.

IMPORTANT:

- GRS (Given, Required & Solution) may be used instead of the GRASS method if the student prefers. GRS is just a condensed version of GRASS, where action, solution and statement are combined in a single part.
- GRS is not the only way to solve a word problem but it is highly recommended.

   3. Draw pictures! This will help you visualize the question.

   For example: What is the area of a carpet that is 50 cm by 30 cm?

   Draw the "carpet" and label the side. With the picture we see that we have both sides of the rectangle and now we can solve the area.

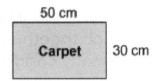

Next ➡

4. Guess and Check

For example: What is x if x + 6 = 25?

Pick different numbers for x and test them out until you get the result you need. Make sure to show all the different numbers you tried.

Let x = 15 → 15 + 6 = 21 (so x = 15 doesn't work)
Let x= 19 → 19 + 6 = 25 (so x = 19 is your answer)

Build your child's confidence in Math!

MATHPROJECT
Empowering minds

At MathProject, we firmly believe that mastering mathematics develops the problem-solving abilities of a child. Our mission is to deliver math education that cultivates 'problem-solvers' who are capable of shaping our future!

Why Us?

- **Personalized Learning Plans**

- **Qualified Teachers**

- **Interactive Sessions**

- **Generous Teaching Hours**

- **Weekly Progress Tracking**

- **5-star Google Reviews**

Our 100% online, virtual program welcomes students of all grade levels, from kindergarten through grade 12, from all over USA and Canada.

What our parents are saying:

My daughter has evolved a lot since she started doing the MathProject one year ago. The teachers are always very kind and patient with her. The school became very easy for her now and her grades are always above 90% in math. Besides, it is online, so no time wasted in traffic or waiting room.
- Marcello Valença

Book a FREE assessment today!

 +1-844-628-4243   www.mathproject.us | www.mathproject.ca

Our Method:

1

Free Skills Assessment
Students begin by taking a free assessment that allows us to assess their current knowledge and skill level.

2

Customized Learning Plan
With a clear understanding of the student's current skill level, our team develops a customized study plan that will ensure each student's progress at their own pace through our curriculum while simultaneously building their confidence and mastery of the concepts.

3

Performance Reviews
Our team continuously monitors a student's progress to ensure they are mastering the concepts. We administer regular tests to verify student progress and skill retention. Parents are informed weekly of the student progress.

Competitor Analysis:

Differentiators	MathProject	Kumon	Mathnasium	Spirit of Math
Maximum Weekly Teaching Hours	1.5 to 6 hours	0.5 hours	2 to 2.5 hours	1.5 hours
Student to Teacher Ratio	3:1	Nil	5:1	20:1
Customized Learning Plan for each Student	Yes	No	Yes	No
Test Prep for Gifted Programs and Math Contests	Yes	No	No	Yes
Unlimited Access to math curriculum and worksheets	Yes	No	No	No
Daily Drop-In Sessions (for math homework help)	Yes	No	No	No
Fostering a relationship with the teacher	Yes	No	No	No
Ongoing timed Assessments and Tests	Yes	No	No	No
Performance (money-back) Guarantee*	Yes	No	No	No

Note: Terms and conditions apply on any guarantees offered. See MathProject website for details.

Book a FREE assessment today!

Call Us: 844-628-4243
www.mathproject.us | www.mathproject.ca

   @mathprojectlearning

Made in the USA
Las Vegas, NV
23 August 2024

94328205R10096